EARL LOVELACE

THE WINE
OF ASTONISHMENT

INTRODUCTION BY MARJORIE THORPE

HEINEMANN

For Jean and Judy

Heinemann International Literature and Textbooks
a division of Heinemann Educational Books Ltd
Halley Court, Jordan Hill, Oxford OX2 8EJ

Heinemann Educational Books Inc
361 Hanover Street, Portsmouth, New Hampshire, 03801, USA

Heinemann Educational Books (Nigeria) Ltd
PMB 5205, Ibadan
Heinemann Kenya Ltd
PO Box 45314, Nairobi, Kenya
Heinemann Educational Boleswa
PO Box 10103, Village Post Office, Gaborone, Botswana

LONDON EDINBURGH MELBOURNE SYDNEY
AUCKLAND SINGAPORE TOKYO MADRID PARIS
HARARE ATHENS BOLOGNA

Series Editor: Adewale Maja-Pearce

British Library Cataloguing in Publication Data
Lovelace, Earl
The wine of astonishment. ——— (Caribbean writers series)
I. Title   II. Series
843[F]   PR9272.9.L6

ISBN 0-435-98880-8

Printed in Great Britain by
Cox and Wyman Ltd, Reading, Berkshire

91 92 93 94 95 10 9 8

CONTENTS

Thou hast shewed thy people hard
things: thou hast made us to drink
the wine of astonishment.

(Psalm 60,3 Authorised Version)

Introduction

MARJORIE THORPE
University of the West Indies
St. Augustine, Trinidad

On 28 November 1917, the Colonial Government passed a law proscribing the religious practices of the Spiritual Baptist Church in Trinidad and Tobago. In presenting the *Shouters Prohibition Ordinance* which allowed local magistrates considerable powers in dealing with this 'trouble', the Attorney General admitted the exceptional character of the bill, and stressed the reluctance of the Government to do anything which interferred with 'the liberty of the individual to choose the way in which he should worship'. Going on to describe the 'exceptional circumstances' which had given rise to the bill, however, the Attorney General argued first, that the Spiritual Baptists constituted an unmitigated nuisance: 'Apparently, the neighbourhood in which a Shouters meeting takes place is made almost impossible for residential occupation'; and, secondly, he observed that the practices of the Baptists were not such 'as should be tolerated in a well-conducted community'.[1]

When Herskovits investigated the Baptist sect more than two decades later, a very different image of the Movement emerged. Whereas the Government had deemed the Shouters a social evil, and had claimed that their meetings were merely the occasion for 'all sorts of indecent acts', Herskovits discovered in the practices of the Shouters nothing more damaging than an example of how 'African worship . . . had been shaped and reinterpreted to fit into the patterns of European worship';[2] and they noted the Shouters' reputation for probity, trustworthiness in personal dealings and high standards of moral conduct.

The prejudice implicit in the *Shouters Prohibition Ordinance* has been attributed primarily to the fact that the possession phenomenon, which distinguishes the sect from other local Christian denominations, offended the establishment's deep-rooted tradition of austere worship:[3] 'This phenomenon consists of the familiar pattern whereby the personality of the devotee is displaced by what is believed to be the

Spirit of the Holy Ghost, which causes the one under possession variously to sing, shout, dance, stamp, prophesy or cure.'[1] To a public striving for 'respectability', as manifested in the social and cultural mores of the white colonial power, the Baptist form of worship appeared particularly repugnant; and the fact that the Movement's membership was also black working-class further explains the hostility of a legislature comprised entirely of nominated members who, either by virtue of their birth or their education, were totally committed to defending the lifestyle of their colonial masters.

In his fourth published novel, *The Wine of Astonishment*, Earl Lovelace charts the history of a Spiritual Baptist community from the passing of the *Prohibition Ordinance* in 1917 until the lifting of the ban in 1951. The choice of subject matter reflects Lovelace's continuing awareness of the vital role of the artist in the de-colonization process. Beginning with the publication of his first novel, *While Gods Are Falling* in 1965, one can discern in Lovelace's fiction an ongoing commitment to 'the task of re-education and regeneration' which, Chinua Achebe has suggested, is one of the first duties of the writer in a post-colonial society.[3] It is a commitment that has consistently influenced the direction of Lovelace's creative energy, encouraging him to explore in his works those experiences which have shaped the social and psychological development of the black West Indian community:

> We have this church in the village. We have this church. The walls make out of mud, the roof covered with carrat leaves: a simple hut with no steeple or cross or acolytes or white priests or latin ceremonies. But is our own. Black people own it . . .
> We have this church where we gather to sing hymns and ring the bell and shout hallelujah and speak in tongues when the Spirit come; and we carry the word to the downtrodden and the forgotten and the lame and the beaten, and we touch black people soul. (p. 32)

As a syncretistic religion, born out of Africa's encounter with Europe in the New World, Lovelace sees in the Spiritual Baptist system of faith and worship, in their 'Africanization of Christianity', a living example of the creative and regenerative impulses inherent in the black creole cultural tradition. The conflict between the Bonasse Spiritual Baptists and the established authorities is therefore conceived as only one other episode in the centuries-old struggle between Prospero and Caliban; and it is this which accounts for the symbolic significance of the church in the world of the novel. In tracing the history of this particular community, Lovelace is reflecting on the more general experience of the black man in the Caribbean. The novel therefore returns us to the now familiar black West Indian world of deprivation and oppression, but with the important distinction that, here, the image of the black West Indian as courageous victim is superseded by the presentation of the black West Indian as authentic hero-figure.

In *The Wine of Astonishment* Lovelace moves away from the third-person narration of his earlier novels, electing instead to relate the events from the point of view of a middle-aged peasant woman who is, herself, a member of the Baptist church. The change has certain obvious advantages. Lovelace's Eva is cast in the tradition of those clear-thinking, resolute and spiritually-resilient mother-figures who have always peopled the world of Caribbean fiction. Thus, although her sympathetic 'inside' view of the Shouter Movement conflicts sharply with the recorded perceptions of the wider society, the associations which she provokes dispose the reader to prefer her authority to that of the establishment's colonial regime. And this authority is further enhanced by Lovelace's linguistic skill which, from the outset, encourages the reader to believe that he is in fact listening to the artless, unstructured narrative of a simple peasant woman:

> God don't give you more than you could bear, I say. 'Cause for hundreds of years we bearing what He send like the earth bear the hot sun and the rains and the dew and the cold, and the earth is still the earth, still here for man to build house on and fall down on, still sending up shoots and flowers and growing things.
>
> But what sin we commit? What deed our fathers or we do that so vex God that He rain tribulation on us for generations? What is it, the children ask, as children will ask . . .
>
> So, I tell them: What God will vex with you for? You ain't do God nothing. God don't vex with his children. (p. 1)

Moreover, Lovelace overcomes the limitation which a first person narrator imposes on the reader's perspective by suggesting quite early the strongly communal character of the church: 'We preach the Word and who have ears to hear, hear . . . [And] after the service finish the brethren could discuss together how the corn growing, how the children doing . . . and the sisters could find out who sick from the congregation so we could go and sit with her a little and help out with the cooking . . . or the washing or the ironing.' (pp. 32–3) Through this device, the motivations of characters other than the narrator are readily revealed. The conversion of Ivan Morton's mother to Roman Catholicism is a case point. More than that, this emphasis on a communal way of life also facilitates the inclusion of events not witnessed by the narrator; and hence the detailed accounts of the Bolo episodes: 'later when things start to happen that involve Bolo, people would talk. Everybody would have a story that he witness, to add to or to take away from others say; so that though it is true that every single body wasn't there to see every single thing that happen to Bolo, we, all of us, know his history just as if we was all there to see.' (p. 87)

The choice of narrator has the further advantage of establishing the tone of the novel as that blend of religious fervour, worldly wisdom and sardonic wit which characterises the black creole woman's response to her environment. In this way, the narrator's rapturous description of 'how we break the law' is counterbalanced by her realistic appraisal of the consequences of the act: 'When you break the law, you don't hurt the law, you don't change the law, you just make the law more law.' (p. 64) Similarly, the matter-of-fact way in which Eulalie's pregnancy is reported deliberately mutes the community's profound sense of violation and betrayal: 'Then a few months after Ivan leave and gone back to Port-of-Spain, Eulalie Clifford wasn't swinging her hips again, because hips don't swing too easy when a girl in the family way. So she had the baby. We was expecting Ivan to put a ring on her finger, if not immediate, at least after he finish his examination, but that magic didn't happen.' (p. 46) Here, the mask of humourous detachment is allowed to slip only once with the mention of the word 'magic', but it is enough to remind the reader of the fundamental tension in the novel between a world-view which affirms the inherent dignity of all men, and a world-view which insists that a man's worth is truly determined by his colour, his social status and his economic power.

Finally, the narrator's supposed political innocence allows Lovelace to probe the immortality and fraudulence of the political system without resorting to invective or losing his highly effective control of tone. Here is Eva's account of Ivan Morton's political successes:

> He get a job for Sister Ruth son, Leon in the Agricultural Station, he assist Aggie with her old age pension, and if you wanted a recommendation, you could go to him and he would give you a paper to carry to the foreman on the road gang. He was doing things. Roads was bad in

Bonasse, he fix some roads. Land was scarce and the government had surveyors surveying the land behind the cemetery to give it out to people, though before we get it we would have to wait until the surveyors finish doing their work. And though one or two complain, we know they didn't build Rome in a day. Things was still hard but the papers was saying things would improve. The government had some people from England making a report to give teachers and civil servants more pay, and a lot of Americans was coming in to put up industries in the island with a tax holiday. (p. 5–6)

As a member of that large, dispossessed black West Indian community, we may assume that Eva is sincere in her praise of Ivan Morton. Certainly, she wants to believe in him, for he is the village boy who has escaped from Bonasse and made good, the hoped-for saviour of his community. But behind Eva's enthusiastic description of Ivan Morton's accomplishments, stands Lovelace, the novelist, making a damning condemnation of West Indian politics and West Indian politicians. Thus, Ivan Morton's declared concern for the villagers is seen to manifest itself in two isolated incidents, at least one of which is a mere exercise in bureaucratic procedure. Again, the reader is invited to contrast the image of the villagers seeking the letters of recommendation which would allow them to work 'on the road gang', fixing *some* roads while waiting to secure land 'behind the cemetery', with the image of the chauffeur-driven Ivan Morton, now ensconced in the abandoned Richardson mansion, assisting his middle-class compatriots to increase the social and economic distance between them and their less 'civilized' fellows. In like manner, the American's 'tax holiday' assumes ironic significance in the context of Buntin's rejected application for a loan to turn his small shop into a grocery. And the final satiric thrust is extended to include the type of irresponsible journalism which uses the written word to perpetuate and validate the values of an invidious and oppressive social system.

Lovelace's criticism of West Indian society emerges most clearly in his delineation of character; and in the person of Ivan Morton he holds up to public scrutiny two figures who have consistently attracted his censure: the uncommitted politician and the apostate schoolmaster. Morton's political career reflects a pattern that has existed as long as the elective process in the Caribbean, and Lovelace's exposé of Morton's political chicanery includes an understanding of the particular circumstances which have encouraged many West Indian politicians to engage in political activity merely as a means of securing upward social mobility. Moreover, since most members of the community approve the rapid social and material advancement that attends Morton's election to the island legislature, Lovelace suggests that the whole society stands implicated in his false system of values.

As a politician, then, Ivan Morton stands accused of social irresponsibility; but it is his betrayal of his moral authority that invites Lovelace's harshest criticism. Because a colonial education was, for a long time, the only means by which a black West Indian could escape the social and economic constraints of his environment and attain prestige in the wider society, the Afro-West Indian has always placed high value on scholastic achievements. And it is to the scholar that the black community has looked for leadership and the formal articulation of their goals and values. Ivan Morton first compromises his moral integrity when he rejects Eulalie in favour of her lighter-skinned rival who speaks Standard English. In the person of Eulalie, Lovelace has imaged the beauty, vitality and wholesomeness of the black creole cultural tradition. Ivan Morton's rejection of her therefore constitutes a profound act of betrayal. The fact that he subsequently abandons his father's house and declares his contempt for the Spiritual Baptist system of worship merely serves to emphasise just how completely he has broken faith with his community and internalized the values of the Prospero world-view.

This theme of betrayal is further developed through the person of Corporal Prince, the brutish policeman. Commenting on the relationship between the police and the Trinidadian lower class in his study, *Social Stratification in Trinidad*, Lloyd Braithwaite observes: 'The "aggresiveness" of the lower class West Indian has frequently been commented upon. What tends to escape the notice of both the Trinidadian of the upper classes and the superficial visitor is the aggression which in a sense is directed *against* the lower class.'[6] Braithwaite continues:

> The acceptance of rioting as endemic in the colonial empire and the use of troops for the purpose of putting down such disturbances was openly recognized in some quarters.
>
> The effect of the need to use the police force as a potential weapon against internal disturbance and external threat led to a policy of exclusive staffing of the officer ranks of the force . . .
>
> The effect of this cleavage . . . meant that the police force . . . had no policy of 'West Indianization'. It also led to a certain distance between officers and men and to a type of discipline which seemed to generate a great deal of hostility against the superior officer. This hostility was denied any institutionalized form of expression for security reasons.

Consequently, a great deal of the aggression generated was expended against the mass of the people.[7]

In the light of this account one might argue that, for all his villainy, Prince is as much the victim of social prejudice as the Spiritual Baptists whom he so willingly persecutes. Lovelace however does not posit the reasons for the corporal's violent aggressiveness. What concerns him here is the fact that such acts of aggression *are* possible, that they are condoned and even encouraged by the authority of the establishment, and that they are perpetuated by members of the same black community. If in Ivan Morton we see the corruption of the black community's political and moral integrity, Corporal Prince's activities warn of the skill with which the colonial powers could subvert and control a people's potential for emancipatory action.

Both Ivan Morton and Prince belong to that category of false heroes whom Lovelace consistently identifies in his fiction. In the figure of Bolo we are reintroduced to another of Lovelace's social groupings: the alienated idealists. This figure first appears in Lovelace's second novel, *The Schoolmaster* (1968), in the person of Benn, the drunken guide. We meet him again in *The Dragon Can't Dance* (1979) in the figure of Fisheye, 'the badjohn' of Calvary Hill. But Bolo is closer to Fisheye than to Benn for, by the end of *The Schoolmaster*, Benn seems to have made the leap of faith which transforms him into an authentic hero-figure. Not so Bolo. Bolo shares with his precursors a lively sense of his own worth and dignity as a human being. He also possesses that courage and personal integrity which distinguishes Lovelace's most sympathetic characters. For men such as these, there can be no compromising with laws and conventions which deny rather than affirm their humanity. But what distinguishes them from Lovelace's hero-figures is the quality of their response to the social realities of their environment. Whereas the suffering which Lovelace's heroes endure becomes the prelude to creative action, the Bolos are seduced into a posture of violent confrontation, directing their destructive rage not only against a hostile establishment, but also against the very people whom they desire to save.

The informing idea behind the creation of all Lovelace's hero-figures is the Christian concept of redemptive suffering. This concept is reflected either in aspects of the plot or in the structure of the novels. It is apparent in *The Schoolmaster* and *The Wine of Astonishment* where we have the Church formally present (in orthodox form in *The Schoolmaster*, in a less orthodox form in *Wine*). But the pattern is also evident in *While Gods are Falling* where the action covers a three-day period, suggestive of the death/resurrection motif, and in *The Dragon Can't Dance* which begins with 'Carnival', a prelude to the Lenten experience of suffering and rebirth.

Lovelace establishes Bee, the hero of *The Wine of Astonishment*, as a Christ-figure at his very first appearance in the novel. The parallel is further developed as Bee struggles to preserve faith in his vision and in his community in the face of betrayal, when it seems that the defeat which he knows as leader of the church and the abasement which he must endure are direct consequences of his commitment to man's higher ideals: 'We shoulda kill Prince' (p. 145). Bee's spiritual conflict is imaged in his struggle with the land: 'I go and find him there in the hot sun . . . standing there with his back wet down with perspiration, lifting up the iron fork in the air and bringing it down and burying it in the earth and turning over the earth and lifting up the fork again, sinking it into the earth with his strength as if it was the earth that hurt him and he wanted to stab it, stab it, stab it until he kill it.' (p. 56.) The sense of bondage and desolation which he experiences is reflected in his physical bearing as he moves with 'that stiff, steady, hurting walk of a man bearing a funeral coffin' (p. 72). Yet Lovelace suggests that Bee's personal experience of Golgotha is critical to his spiritual development, for it constitutes the testing ground which discovers both to himself and to his community the superior quality of his faith, and the breadth of his compassion. And it is these qualities which distinguish Bee from Bolo. Whereas Bolo succumbs to the evil in the community, Bee turns defeat into triumph by refusing to betray his nobler impulses. The ending of the novel is a comment on the value of this response.

The Wine of Astonishment celebrates a people's struggle to achieve freedom, and to assert their dignity as human beings. It speaks to the oppressed, everywhere.

Notes

1 Quoted by Melville J. Herskovits and Frances S. Herskovits in *Trinidad Village* (New York: Alfred A. Knopf, 1947), pp. 324–44.

2 *Ibid*, p. vi.

3 Albert Gomes, *Through a Maze of Colour* (Trinidad: Key Caribbean Publications, 1974), p. 78.

4 Herskovits, *op. cit.*, p. 183.

5 Chinua Achebe, 'The Novelist as Teacher' in *Morning Yet on Creation Day* (London: Heinemann, 1975), p. 45.

6 Lloyd Braithwaite, *Social Stratification in Trinidad* (Jamaica: ISER, 1975), p. 131.

7 *Ibid*, p. 132.

1 Bee Goes to See Ivan Morton

God don't give you more than you can bear, I say. 'Cause for hundreds of years we bearing what He send like the earth bear the hot sun and the rains and the dew and the cold, and the earth is still the earth, still here for man to build house on and fall down on, still sending up shoots and flowers and growing things.

But what sin we commit? What deed our fathers or we do that so vex God that He rain tribulation on us for generations? What is it, the children ask, as children will ask who don't know, who open their eyes in a world where the food never 'nuff and the house falling down and the police in we tail and the magistrate trembling to send us to jail, who see us carrying on our shoulders a load more heavy than anybody else own.

So I tell them: What God will vex with you for? You ain't do God nothing. God don't vex with his children.

But children ain't fools. They have their own eyes. They know; so they sit down on the bench in the kitchen watching me, waiting for me to tell them more. For if God ain't vex with us then why we alone have to carry this heavy burden? And Bee there too, standing up by the kitchen door, with his two hands stretch out across the door like how Jesus Christ had his hands when they crucify him on the cross, and his face half turned to me, listening, as if what I have to tell the children is for him too.

So I tell them:

Is because we could bear it. Is because out of all the

1

shoulders in the world our shoulders could bear more weight. and out of all the flesh in the world, our flesh could hold more pain, and out of all the hearts in the world our heart could stomach more ache, without breaking or burning or bursting, than any shoulder or flesh or heart. For God ain't made this world by guess. Things have meaning. And this sea and this earth that will bury us all and the wind and the sun and not one o' them pretty little stars ain't come by whistling. God have His reasons for everything. He have eyes, and all man have here is the few moments that God give him and a little sense to learn who he is and why, so he could make use of his little time here and praise God and die. The strong suffer most, the weak dies.

'And if He give us this . . . If He give you this, Reggie,' I tell my last boychild, 'is because you . . . we could bear it and rise.'

'We could bear it?' Bee say, coming alive in front the door. 'We could bear it? From the police and from the magistrate we could bear it. But from our own people? Our own? To put a man in the Council and have to bear it from him too. . . ?'

'We could bear it, and rise,' I say, looking straight at Reggie, 'so don't cry. Don't cry because you fail this examination. Your life still in front of you.'

But Reggie was crying. All the fuss we make about this examination. All this fuss. 'Boy, you alive,' I tell him. And his sisters on the bench next to him sit down silent with their face long, witnessing with him this tribulation.

'Ma, maybe Mr Morton could do something to help Reggie,' Joyce say.

'Maybe, chile,' I say. 'Maybe.'

'Six months!' Bee say, taking himself down from the cross in front the door. 'Six months now Ivan Morton in the Council and he ain't do nothing to make the church free. Six months! You expect him to do something for this boy?'

'You have to give him a little time, Bee.' I say. 'He's a new man in the Council; six months ain't nutten. And we could wait; things not going too bad with the church: the police ain't troubling us much again, and we worship and pray, not in the real way, true, but we worship and pray.'

'And every other day we growing more away, going more astray from ourself. Why you think we put him there?' Bee say.

'Six months ain't nutten, Bee. Six months is just a hour, a minute these days. The man new, now learning what to do. You have to give him time.'

'Time!' Bee say, and he scratch his head and he shift his body and turn his face to the road where the evening going down and the children by the standpipe making a racket, laughing and clashing their buckets as they jostle each other to catch water. 'Time!'

'Six months ain't much, Bee,' I say, trying to make my voice calm. 'And Ivan Morton live right there up the street not far from here. You could go and talk to him any time.'

Bee sigh and Bee groan and Bee shake his head and put up his arms back on the cross like Jesus crucify in front the door.

'Even a child does take more than six months to born,' I say.

Bee, with his hand jam against the door, turn and look at me and the children as if he is a spider trap in its web, and maybe he want to say to hell with the church, to hell with Ivan Morton, to hell with everything, but he can't get out the web, he must go on hoping.

'Six months,' he say, thinking, and he sigh. 'Six months ain't really so long you know.' And he look at me and try to smile and to hold his patience and to wait.

'T'ain't so long,' I say, making my voice light too; for I know Bee, I know he want to believe in Ivan Morton. He want to believe . . . and I want to believe too.

Two months pass. Evening. I in the kitchen over the mortar pounding plantains for us to eat with the steam fish on the fire

3

cooking, and my mind far away to Port of Spain or wherever my two big boy children is. Now and again I hear from Winston, but from Taffy not a word, not a message by a friend, a letter, nothing, so I don't know if he dead or sick or in jail. I don't know nothing.

Evening, as I say. I sit down on the stool in front the mortar, lifting the pestle and watching my hands bring it down to crush the plantains lying down there to take the pounding that will break them down, mix them up and make them stiff and good for eating; and I wondering if the world is a mortar and we is the plantains below the pestle, taking the pounding.

Then, sudden, to interrupt my thinking, Joyce full, high screaming voice reach me, have me wondering who killing who as I go rushing outside to see what happening. But there she is leaning over the window, pointing up the street, and when I look all I could see is the tail of a cream motor car, taking up the whole road, going round the corner out of sight.

'You see it, Ma!' Joyce say.

'See what? The car?'

'Yes.'

'Is a car you call me out here to see, girl? I coulda swear somebody dead. You think I ain't have nothing to do but rush outside to see a motor car?'

'Clyde driving it,' she say.

'So Clyde driving a car.'

'Is Mr Morton car.'

'Another car?'

So that night, I tell Bee: 'New car!'

'What you want the man to do? Now that they make him a minister he must live according to his position. What so wrong about a new car?'

'Okay! Okay!' I say, because I don't want to make an argument over Ivan Morton; I want to believe too just like Bee. I want to believe in Ivan Morton.

Now in Bonasse we seeing Ivan Morton passing by in his new car, a lord in the back seat in his jacket and tie, his head tilt to one side and his face halfway between seriousness and a little bit of a smile. He fix his elbows on the hand-rest near the window and the same two fingers he lift to hold up in a V for victory sign, he rest against his cheek like those screen stars in the magazine I see Joyce reading.

Oh, those days he popular: children running behind his car calling his name, and the women holding up their babies so Ivan Morton could see them, for a glance from him is a blessing. Through the glass of the window of his car he watch us (I there too) and he wave, moving one hand across and just in front his face like a Catholic priest blessing his congregation, giving a thrill to all we poor women who have children and see him as the saviour who footsteps we want our boy children to follow in.

'He looking so nice,' people say.

'He sweet eh, chile,' the women say.

And all about people was naming their new boy children Ivan and when Simmons had a daughter they gave her the name Ivana. His office was pack with people in those days. Mostly they wanted work or a recommendation to get a loan or a piece of land and though he couldn't help everybody, he do the best he could. He get a job for Sister Ruth son, Leon, in the Agricultural Station, he assist Aggie with her old age pension, and if you wanted a recommendation, you could go to him and he would give you a paper to carry to the foreman on the road gang. He was doing things. Roads was bad in Bonasse, he fix some roads. Land was scarce and the government had survey-ors surveying the land behind the cemetery to give it out to people, though before we get it we would have to wait until the surveyors finish doing their work. And though one or two complain, we know they didn't build Rome in a day. Things was still hard but the papers was saying things would improve.

The government had some people from England making a report to give teachers and civil servants more pay, and a lot of Americans was coming in to put up industries in the island with a tax holiday.

New schools was building, giving more children places in high school, and we was hearing that soon there would be free secondary education on the whole island. I wanted to go and ask Mr Morton to see if he could do something to get Reggie in college, but Bee say no. 'What would happen if everybody went to the minister to get his child in college? What would happen?' Bee ask me. And though I tell him that everybody was going to Ivan Morton for their own personal business, Bee refuse to be one of them, even though time was passing and Reggie, in seventh standard, was getting too big for short pants. But I guess is so things go. The people who work most hardest for Ivan Morton in the election, they was getting nothing.

Take Mr Buntin. He wanted to borrow some money to turn his little shop into a grocery store so he could sell things like Chin. He couldn't get a loan from the bank because as you know they don't lend out their money to black people. Portuguese, Syrian, Chinee, okay, but black people is a different story; so when the bank turn him down, Buntin went to Ivan Morton to see if he could get the government to help him as how they was helping industries with a tax holiday. I don't know the full story: what questions Buntin couldn't answer, what security he didn't have. Buntin didn't get the loan. Buntin himself didn't talk about it too much. He wasn't happy, but he didn't make a big fuss about it. As he himself say to Bee: 'Is not that I ain't vex about it, but we have him there, we have to support him. Those who against us in this island would love to see us quarrelling and ridiculing one another; I, for one, not going to give them that satisfaction. Leave him alone. Give him time, Brother Bee . . .'

It was right after Ivan Morton come back from his trip to England. I remember Bee face, sitting that evening under the mango tree, looking at a newspaper where Ivan Morton was in a winter coat and a hat, his hands in his pocket, stand up next to a statue of a half-naked woman. 'He went to see the Queen of England to talk to her about changing the law,' Bee tell me. I could see his face that evening and I could hear his voice trying more to convince himself than to convert me. It was right after that, the same week in fact, the day after Clarissa daughter had the baby who was going to be my God-daughter. I went down to the shop and when I come back just before dark, I meet Joyce in the kitchen making dinner. I hardly had time to sit down and catch my breath.

'They moving, you know,' Joyce tell me.

'Who?'

'Mr Morton.'

'Girl,' I tell her. 'Where you get your gossip from? What Ivan Morton will move for? His father leave a house for him and he is right here with his own people. He getting a good salary so he could fix up his house, make it look nice with a flower garden and a hibiscus hedge and a lawn like any of those big shot houses. What he will move for?'

'Ma, but Clyde say . . .'

'Clyde! Clyde! Girl, I hope you watching yourself with that Clyde, you hear.' And she smile that smile that know and don't know, that sweetheart, young lady smile, shy and full up with all that soft, dangerous kind of knowing that girls with growing breasts begin to know, so I figure she done gone past one step with Clyde, what step I don't know, for young girls in their mother house have their own private business for them alone. Yes, love is sweet, love is fine, but children blood get hot too, and what sweet in the mouth does burn another part. So though this Clyde is a nice boy – what boy who have twenty-three years and have his heart on a girl and does drive a new,

7

clean car even though it ain't his own, holding his hand over the window to wave at her when he pass – what young man like that ain't a nice boy? But nice boy ain't no recommendation in certain things, and a mother is a fool not to warn a daughter to be careful until the time reach when she know the girl could be full and have somebody by her side to care.

'You better watch yourself with Clyde, you hear?'

And Joyce stand up looking at me with her face flowering in a smile, as if I too old and never feel and can't know and she is the first girl in the world that sit down in the evening by a window watching the road for a boy to pass and wave at her and flutter her heart.

'So what it is Clyde say?' For now I want to know, because if anybody is to know what Ivan Morton doing, it must be Clyde, because Clyde chauffeuring Ivan Morton all over the place.

'The big house. He moving to the big house.'

Clyde really should know; but, the big house?

The big house is a old mansion of brick and stone that stand up on top of Bonasse hill looking over the sea and the whole village. A tall, white building with stain glass windows, it was big, bigger than any house in Bonasse, bigger than any house I ever see black people live in, big nearly as the Catholic church, a house lived in for ages by generations of Richardsons, old now, since Richardson gone back to England and leave it, the walls crack and stain with age, quiet too, and when the wind blow, you could hear the three giant palmiste trees rustling, whispering like spirits. It was a haunted house they say, behind it was a graveyard with the grey tombs under the red bougainvillaea tree, holding generations of dead Richardsons. The American man who buy over the Estate from Richardson didn't want to have nothing to do with it. It like a old church with God gone from it that nobody want any more to worship in.

'Ivan Morton will never live there,' I tell Joyce. 'I don't care what Clyde say. No.'

'But, Ma . . .'

'I don't care what Clyde say,' I say.

That same evening I talk to Bee.

'Ivan Morton moving up to Mr Richardson big house, you know.'

And Bee fixing to eat the bake and saltfish! 'I know.'

Not another word. I didn't say another word. I guess Bee understand what that mean.

'Eva,' Bee say, as if he know what I was thinking, 'Ivan Morton want to make himself a man for people to recognize and if it mean going to live in that house, he will do it. That don't mean he will turn against his people. That don't mean he will forsake us, Eva.'

'What it mean, then?'

'It mean . . . well, he's a big man, educated. It mean he could live like white people. It mean . . .'

'Don't tell me, Bee,' I say. 'Don't tell me.'

I see plenty people move from one house to another, but I never see a kind of moving as when Ivan Morton and his wife leave the village. I know people does move with their belongings, the things they accumulate over the years. Chairs and tables could be old but they belong to you, they is part of you; they is you; you accustom to them and they accustom to you; they is like your own children; you just can't leave them when you moving.

Ivan Morton moved and ain't take one single thing. He and his wife leave the house that his father build with his own two hands – and it wasn't easy for Mr Fitzie. He spend his whole life on it. And it wasn't bad. It could extend. It could fix. This man, Ivan, the son, come now and leave the house as if it was nothing more than a place he was in; worse, as if it was a prison or a hotel where you go in and don't own nothing, just a place where you was staying. They didn't carry table, they didn't

9

carry bed; they didn't even hire a truck to move them.

People say that they had new things to go to in Richardson house is why they abandon everything, but is not a matter of new things: is wickedness and a sin. Money is not everything, and new things get old too. Wasn't even as if they was going to meet new things either. Richardson house had old things, dead things, things that generations of Richardson people use: the piano couldn't even play again, and the very house itself was falling down. No, no, no. It was wickedness and a shame. It was as if Ivan Morton was saying to the world that the house his father leave him was nothing, and his father life was nothing and his mother was nothing. Oh Jesus! It *was* a real shame and a disgrace. I poor. I have my few old things that live with me over the years. Don't tell me that I would give them up just so. Is not even as if they give the things to a brother or a sister or a aunt or even a friend, somebody, anybody: they just abandon them like how some women abandon their children, as how some children leave their old parents to beg their bread.

I watch them move – if move is the word. Clyde come and take them in the car with a few trunks of clothes and some books, and they was gone. We see it, me and Bee and the children, from where we was living. We watch them drive away. We watch them go. And now Bee know he can't make no more excuse to himself about Ivan Morton.

'I will go and see him,' Bee say.

But he will wait as the whole village wait, because this is our own boy, son of the soil, our hope, man to save the people, and we want to give him every chance to be true. Then one evening, the police raid the church. We wasn't doing nothing against the law, and they didn't arrest anybody, but the police had raid the church, and we had a man in the Council.

So Bee go and see Ivan Morton. Not to his house like a friend come to pay a visit; not as a man who with his own time and strength and money, little as it is, campaign the length and breadth of Bonasse and go all through Charlotte and St John's, talking till his voice hoarse, staying up nights till his eyes red to get people to vote for Ivan Morton, so that now Ivan Morton would come to be sitting down in the Legislative Council and have car and chauffeur and big house and forget Bee. Bee go to see him just as if he, Bee, was a ordinary man who didn't make any special effort to see Ivan Morton reach where he reach.

And Bee not vex. He cool. He slow. He putting down his foot, one today, one tomorrow, in the morning sunshine, with his head bend to one side as if a great sorrow pushing it down, but calm, as if he know what he going to tell Ivan Morton when he see him. I stand up and watch him go.

And while he gone that morning, the postman come home and bring a letter. The letter is from the principal of the high school in Charlotte that Reggie, unknowing to his father or me, apply to go to. The letter is asking us to send Reggie to the school. I look at the letter and I think: like this letter come just in time to show me, to show Bee if he was here to receive it, to show us that life going on, that things happening and the children getting big and we getting down in years.

I sit down on the front steps with the letter in my hand, and my eyes looking through the green spaces between the coconut trees to the sky over the sea where gulls circling and dipping like kites, and I think how life so short and how we have to be so strong and I think about the children, the big boys gone away and the little ones here, and I pray for all of them, that they grow up tall and find the strength to bear the tribulation tumbling down on us from generation to generation, especially when you don't have education. Gem, the teacher say, is bright in school, she may be the one to win an exhibition, especially now that they giving more places, though I did prefer that Reggie win one seeing that he is a boy and a boy is a man and a man have the burden of the world on his shoulders in a way that a woman don't, can't have it. And I hear Joyce in the

11

bathroom in the yard, singing with all her voice, and the water splashing. These days she and Clyde going strong. One week they in love: they cooing and sho-shooing, smiling soft and sitting down quiet, making one shadow at the bottom of the steps in the moonlight; next week they not talking to one another; then they back again like ring and finger. Modern love, they say. What modern about that? A man and a woman spar and push each other until they decide who going to rule who, and between Joyce and Clyde is a good battle.

A quiet morning, the smaller children gone to school, and now I there in the kitchen where the split pea boiling. The sun bright and the wind blowing strong from the sea, flapping the open window over the children bedroom. Bee reach back home, his shadow long on the ground in front him, his face swell up like a frog that take all the stones the boys pelt it with and if it get hit once again will burst. I watch Bee. I don't ask him anything. I don't know what word to begin with, what tone to use. He sit down. He ain't say nothing. Then he see the letter that the postman bring where I rest it on the ledge in the kitchen. So I tell him: 'They send for Reggie to go to high school.'

He reach out his hand, take down the letter, open it, and as he read it his face come down a little from the mountain. He look at me. He look away, and I know the words in him to say, but I know there is things that words can't say.

I talk again: 'Reggie will be fourteen just now. If he is to go to high school at all, is best we send him now.'

Bee eyes wander all over the kitchen, and he ain't look at me. He shift a little on the bench and his voice take on a kind of strain as if what he going to say is too heavy for him, have me straining too, like when you watching a man take up a too heavy load, in your mind you straining with the load too.

'Eva, that Ivan Morton look at me and ask what I want to worship as Baptist for. That jackass ask me that. Give me a long lecture about how he up there trying his best to lift his people out of darkness and how – listen to this – how he surprise that a man like me who support him so strong in the election could still hold on to that backward suggestion that the law should change to allow us to worship as heathen.

'Tell me he not against the principle of the freedom of worship but what worrying him is that I, we should still be in the dark ages in these modern times when we could settle down and be civilize.'

'Bee . . .'

'And Mr Civilize sit down there in the whiteman house on the whiteman chair with the whiteman tie and cuff-links and wristwatch on telling me: "We can't change our colour, Dorcas, but we can change our attitude. We can't be white, but we can act white." And all I want is to worship God in my way.'

Bee sit down there in the kitchen and draw a deep breath like he pulling in the whole world through his wide nostrils, and he look sad. I wish that the big boys was home, that the children was around so he could see them, how they growing, how life going on all the time. I wish at that moment they coulda all come warm into the room, not especially to tell him anything, but for him to see them, see life in them.

And because I think I know how hard it is when a man spend his life looking for something, fighting for it, and some fool come and stand between him and it, my heart get full for Bee. I tell him: 'Bee, boy, we still have the children, and we still have some years left and health and strength. If God give us this is because we could bear it. If He choose us for this, we must remember He choose out Jesus, His one and only son, to come down on earth for fools to crucify, and it wasn't because He didn't love Jesus, but because out of all the angels in heaven was only Jesus who had the strength and the beauty and the greatness and the humbleness to come down to earth and

13

become weak like man and bear the world pain and the vinegar and the crown of thorns and still come back again after they nail up His hands and feet on the cross and stab Him with a spear and turn and say: "Father, forgive them. Forgive them!"'

'Forgive?' Bee groan. He look at the letter in his hands. As if he remember something, he say, 'Send him high school. Band your belly and pay for this boy to go high school so they will learn him to turn his back on his family, so they will teach him to act civilize like Ivan Morton? Eh?'

'You can't know that, Bee. Give the boy a chance. The fees ain't too much. Give him a chance.'

'But ... but look at these fellows, eh. Look at them! So civilize they forget where they come from. So civilize they looking at you as if you is nothing, as if your dreams and hopes and life is nothing. So civilize they can't even break a proper fart."

'Maybe is the house and car that turn him so. Maybe.' And I remain wondering what to say – 'Maybe he will change, Bee.'

'Change? Is we who will have to change. Those fellows too civilize to change. That's what wrong with this generation of niggers who went to school. Get so blasted civilize they get stupid. Stupid! Crosby sacrifice and send his son to school in England. The boy come back home for a few days holiday, see some crabs Crosby have in a barrel. This is the son: "Dad, what are those thangs there?" Talking like Englishman. Crosby ain't tell him nothing. When he poke his finger in the barrel and the crab catch hold of him, he bawl: "Pa! The crab! The crab!" A well educated boy, yes. Lawyer, economist or something.'

And I there smiling at his joke that ain't no joke, but glad for a chance to smile so Bee could smile too and ease out of his mood. But Bee ain't smiling yet. I feel so helpless. I say, 'You try, Bee. You try, man. You do your part.'

This time Bee smile and sigh and lean back on the bench, passing his hand backward and forward over his hair. 'My part, eh?' And he smile. 'Eva, how many years we married? Twenty-three years, not so? A long time, eh? You think because I don't talk about it, I don't see, I don't know? Things you want to have in your house like other people – a radio, good chairs . . .'

'What happen to the chairs we have here?'

'Things for you to wear. Dress, a new hat, and to go somewhere out of this kitchen for a change. A show in San Fernando. To see a picture. You think I don't know?'

'We make out, Bee.'

'. . . and the children. You think I don't know that they want things too?'

'We don't complain. We let what we have do, and we better off than plenty people.'

'. . . and if tomorrow something should happen to me, what I will leave for you all? The house and all want fixing.'

'What you worrying yourself for, man? We starving? We naked? We sick? We don't have a place to sleep? What you worrying yourself for?'

And Bee hold down his head, looking at his hands holding on to the side of the bench he was sitting on. I watch and see the muscles on his arms as his fingers grip the bench.

'Bee? Bee! Ain't we always come through? Eh, Bee? Ain't we always come through? We is London, boy. Remember the war days when the Germans was bombing London and the people use to say, London can take it. Remember? We is London.'

Bee raise his head, his eyes look at me, and he smile a smile that this time break through his sadness and make him look nice and funny and like a little boy. 'London? London is joke to we. We take so much bombing for so long. We take so much

15

bullets. All around. Back and front. Up and down. London? London never feel what we feel.'

And Bee sit down there with the letter in one hand, tapping his foot on the floor, nodding his head, smiling this funny smile and feeling what London never feel.

I go and sit down on the bench next to him, and I hold his hands: 'Let us send the boy to high school, Bee,' I say.

And Bee there nodding his head and tapping his foot, the smile still on his face.

'Eh, Bee? You going to let him go?'

And he nod his head yes. 'We could bear it,' he say. 'The world is not a marketplace where you quarrel over the price you have to pay. God fix the price already, and if we could pay ours, we have to be thankful. Things have meaning.'

And Bee get up and walk to the door and I hear in his voice the breaking and doubting and hoping and just like that I hear a song and I was singing:

> '*I never get weary yet*
> *I never get weary yet*
> *Forty long years I work in the field*
> *And I never get weary yet.*'

And my heart give a little skip as Bee join in, and the two of us was singing.

Lord, you make your people see hard things, you make us to drink the wine of astonishment. What to say? But it wasn't over yet; we had more wine to drink in the new year, for in the church that Sunday, rising like a spear out of the back row, with the rest of the congregation, to sing the first hymn, was Bolo. With a new kind of toughness about him, a warrior still, with his chest up and his eyes bright with dreams that fill him, Bolo stand up there with a sunshine smile bursting on his face and his warm spirit brimming out of him to all of us, touching us, joining us with him. And we – when we open our mouths, it was to sing the hymn in the same lawful way, the same dead way, without bellringing or handclapping or shouting.

Bolo stand up there, his lower jaw dropping out his face, his eyes disbelieving, his head turning to look at Bee, at me, at all of us as if he can't believe that after all these years this is where we is. He stand up there in the church, in the midst of our hymn singing, with amazement and heartbreak in his face. Then gradual, as a man who realize he come to the wrong place, he straighten himself up to a height and look down on us, taking back from us his sunshine spirit, holding it to himself and rising above us to the tallness of a judge, to another self, tougher and harder. And I, not bearing to meet his eyes, turn my head away and try to raise another hymn to show him that we still here, still holding on, battling, hoping that tomorrow would be a better day; but when I look back for him, he wasn't there, was gone. He would never come back to our church again.

And how all this come to happen.

2 The War Still Fighting

That year the great war against Japan and the Germans was still fighting. The American soldiers who come down to Trinidad to protect us from invasion was still in Bonasse, drinking Cockspur rum and fulling up the women, driving their jeeps and screeching their brakes like madmen all over the place, waking Christian people up at all hours of the night to hear bottles crash and women scream and guns shoot off and make Bee curse the day that these heathen people land in this colony with money in their pocket and guns on their waist to have mother and daughter whoring down the place and big men touts behind the Yankee dollar.

That was the year when rice was rationing and bread-fruit was king and Bee, working the piece of land behind the cemetery, was able to make a penny or two, because food was scarce and nobody want to plant again, nobody want to fish; everybody want a job on the American Base where they could do nothing whole week and on Friday stretch out their hand and draw a fat pay, like Mitchell, my cousin, who leave off labouring on Richardson Estate, borrow a saw and hammer and pass himself off to the Americans as a carpenter, spend, as he boast forever after, six months carpentering without ever driving a nail. Say how he meet up with this damn fool officer who with no enemy in Trinidad to fight decide to write a book about what he, the American, call Voodoo, and choose Mitchell out to give him information; so that Mitchell, who I never hear talk about nothing more mysterious than food in his belly, is suddenly this big expert on this voodoo, start to tell this fellar – Bob, Mitchell say his name is – all about the different charms man does use to command woman to fall in love with them, and what people have to do to turn yourself from human to animal, or to make yourself into a ball of fire to fly from house to house to suck people blood, the way soucouyants suppose to do. So now poor Bob, feeling that Mitchell really know all these great secrets, frighten that Mitchell use some voodoo on him, allow Mitchell to do exactly as he please, and what Mitchell please to do is to not work.

In no time at all Mitchell is foreman of a gang of carpenters. He is money-lender and Contact Man, dealing in blackmarket goods and selling GI boots and other things that he thief from the American Base. Now he about Bonasse, with a gold ring on every finger, his belt slacken at his waist, his eyes looking at everything like it have a price he could afford to pay. He busy up and down the streets, following where the men go who owe him money: in the dice game behind Chin shop and down the bay at Buntin where the men drink on an evening. Get so fresh and outa place, he want to pinch every woman he meet, and when she open her mouth to disagree, he wave a five dollar bill in her face; and he have the gall to come and boast to Bee, 'Look at me, Bee! Look where I reach! Why you don't leave this hard land you killing yourself on and let me get a job for you with the Americans?' If it wasn't for this war Mitchell would be nobody. Bee don't like this war.

Bolo don't like it either. The seven years before the war, Bolo was in Bonasse, the champion stickfighter, the king, leading the village in battles down the length and breadth of the island; and though he work as a coconut picker on Richardson Estate, making at most sixty-five cents a day from climbing tall coconut trees, with a length of rope round his feet and a sharp cutlass grip between his teeth, he couldn't walk down a Bonasse street if somebody didn't call him for a drink, or call out his name just so – just for the pleasure, just to be able to claim that he is a friend of Bolo, the stickfight king; and you must understand, women didn't leave him alone either.

Oh, was to see him on pay-day Saturday, coming tall, perspiring, his chest unbutton, in the bright sun down Main Street, stopping to wave or make a joke with whoever call out to him. The market women always call out to him, and he would come over to us to the market stalls by the roadside where we was selling, and full with mischief and laughing, he would circle in his arms the first two or three of us to meet him, the rest of us rushing forward to seize hold of one of his hands to show our jealousy, to pretend to be fighting over him.

'Woman, let go my man!'

'No! This man belong to me.'

Or we would turn on him, 'Bolo, how much woman you want? Boy, why you don't get married and stop tantalising the female sex in this village?'

'Who you want him to married?'

And just to see how his eyes would flash before he managed to cover up his feelings, we would say the name of the one girl we know his heart belong to. And with a little laugh, he would turn quick to hug Mother Ruby, the oldest vendor, her headtie wrap in the Martiniquan style, her dress down to her ankles over the thin frame of her bones. 'This girl here is the one I want to marry. Only problem is I don't know how to handle the competition from the other men,' making Mother Ruby get young right away, her eyes wrinkling, flashing, and her two only teeth showing. 'Let me tell you then,' winking at us and drawing down his face to her lips to whisper some scandal in his ear, to kill him, to make him back away from her, 'Ruby! What it is you say?' Mother Ruby choking on her own laughter, and all of us asking innocent, 'What it is she tell you? What she say?'

And he was a comic strip when he ready, staring silent at

glum Sister Lucy, who didn't like nobody, until she gave a smile; or he would roll his eyes at the thick-fleshed Miss Ellen with her big, big eyes and trembling behind among the ochroes and ripe bananas she was selling, asking her how good was her man doing his duty, telling her that if he, the husband, not able, he was willing to give a helping hand; Miss Ellen saying with her own wickedness, her hands akimbo showing the Trojan size of her body, 'You think *you* able?' And he answering in a little boy voice of mockery, 'I will try, Miss Ellen.'

Oh, we had a time with him those mornings, until at last our faces tired and our eyes running water from so much laughing, we would push him away, 'Go way, Bolo. Go way. You no good. We can't talk with you again.'

And when at last he was leaving, each one of us would have something to offer him, a yellow yam, tomatoes, a hand of ripe plantains, things we wouldn't let him refuse; for this Bolo was a special man; and not only to us, the women, to everybody. If you have a house to build or a dead to bury, you could call him to lend a hand, and though he's a man who fears nobody, he knows how to laugh, and if you down to cheer you up, and he could feel sorry.

I, myself, never see him in a stickfight battle cause from young I never go down the bay to the place in front of Buntin shop, the gayelle, where in the season for stickfighting two men alone from all the rest face each other in the ring, with three drums beating and the chantwells singing battle chants to get men brave, to rush the blood into their head and make every one of them want to take up a stick and enter the ring. But I didn't have to go. The whole village talk 'bout him. They say that in the stickfight ring, the gayelle, it don't have a man to stand up in front of him. They say he don't fight just to win battles for himself, for him stickfighting was more the dance, the adventure, the ceremony to show off the beauty of the warrior. And he do it with love and respect, more as if he was

21

making a gift of himself, offering himself up with his quick speed and rhythm, as if what he really want was for people to see in him a beauty that wasn't his alone, was theirs, ours, to let us know that we in this wilderness country was people too, with drums and song and warriors.

But the war come and all stickfight finish, done. The war come and the Government put a ban on Carnival, the grand festival that was the occasion for stickfight contests throughout the island. So for three years now the gayelle empty and the closest you get to a stickfight is maybe on a hot Saturday evening when two old men drinking a rum with their comrades and remembering their warrior days, hearing in their ears the beat of drums and the battle songs, go out onto the rumshop floor and put on a mock battle, their handkerchiefs the weapons, their comrades the chantwells and the rumshop table the drums. New things take over Bonasse. Since the Americans come money start to flow, fellars spring up from nowhere with clean fingernails and pointy tip shoes; lean fellars in zoot suits with long silver chains looping from the fob of their trousers to their side pocket, who, to see their eyes, you have to lift up their hat brims. What women see in them, I don't know; but these was the new heroes. And now, men who used to be dying for Bolo to take a drink with them was passing him in the street without a word of greeting. Bolo feel it. He feel it.

Most evenings he would go down to Buntin shop where the men congregate to play draughts, and he would drink a rum with Clem and listen to the men talk about Hitler, the war and Churchill.

Clem is a chantwell, a singer leading stickfight chants and bongo songs and he could sing a nice sentimental, like Bing Crosby. Clem always had his guitar with him. And he would sit down there picking his guitar above the talking, watching with Bolo what all of us was seeing: the Yankees zooming about the place, the village girls parading, stepping out in high heel

THE WAR STILL FIGHTING

shoes they ain't learn yet to walk in, their dress sticking up against their flesh, their lips paint red and their eyes full with the sickness for money that was the disease taking over everybody. Eulalie was one of them now, she not bright and innocent as when she was seventeen, but she pretty still, and her eyes have this look, as if she discover that life is more tough than she did imagine, and that she is more tougher than she did believe. Eulalie is like the star girl on the movie screen, she belong and yet she different from the other girls. Her shoe heels look higher and her lipstick more red and her dress like it melt down to make one with her skin. You see her and rightaway you think, 'What this girl doing here?' And a sadness strike you. So that sometimes when Bolo stop to talk to us in the market, we say to him, 'Man, why you don't go and take that girl outa that thing? Why you don't go and untangle her from the soldiers?' But that is not a simple story. You will hear it when we come to it.

From where he sit in Buntin shop, Bolo see Eulalie pass, going with whatever man she going with, and he would light a cigarette and look at Clem, and Clem would look at him. Clem could make up a song on anything, and the two of them would sit there with Clem strumming his guitar, making up songs about the village girls and the soldiers and the hustlers as it was happening; and sometimes Clem wouldn't sing at all, just sit with his head lean to one side, the way I see him sometimes when I passing, his fingers pulling soft hard notes out from the guitar strings to match the things that was happening; for it wasn't only the girls, it was the men. Men born here in the village was coming in from the Estate and the sea, barefoot, slow, not so sure that they have a welcome there at Buntin any more; and, with the hustlers jostling them, they would make their way to the counter, and in a voice you could scarcely hear, call for their one sweet burning drink of white rum and drink it down in one swallow. These men look at Bolo as they turn to leave and their eyes would tell him something, and Bolo would go to say a word, but his mouth would remain hanging open, cause he didn't know what to say; and Clem, feeling how hard these things hit Bolo, would change the tempo of his playing, strumming on his guitar the stickfight tunes, keeping in them the beat of battle, but slowing them down to bring out the sound, the cry, the tall sorrow that was flowing in that time, so that men playing draughts – and Bee was one of them too – stop their game and listen.

Then something start to happen. The new men, those with long fingernails, hear the music, something new, something that touch them in some way and they start to crowd around Clem and Bolo to listen whenever Clem start singing, and they would buy a bottle of rum for the table and join in the singing, and sometimes the talk would turn to stickfighting, and they'd ask Bolo a lot of stupid questions about stickfighting that Bolo didn't want to answer. For to these strangers, Bolo is not the Bolo he is to us.

Clem is different. He is more free, more open. To him people is people. In no time Clem had take over telling of stickfight battles and letting them know that Bolo is a stickfight hero. So now Clem and Bolo was the show at Buntin. With all the singing and songs and drinking around them, with the men drumming on the tables, two fellars, wanting to make their own display, would go on to the rumshop floor to battle, with handkerchiefs for sticks. They'd beg Bolo to go in, but Bolo wouldn't go, until one day the Spirit fly to his head and he jump in, dancing, Bee say, with a sadness and a loss too, and a smooth tallness that bring water to the eyes of those who remember him in a real battle; but all the men wanted was to have fun. And, seeing Bolo out on the floor, fellars who never put foot in a real gayelle, who never face the danger of a real battle, glad to face now at no cost, the king, the best, take out handkerchiefs and rush at him so that afterwards they could boast that they played against the champion.

Every day this crowd of fellars was getting more bigger. And more rum was drinking and noise was making. And more and more Bolo was doing this mock stickfighting, as if he was trying to dance back something that was going away. But, according to Clem, Bolo was never happy with those sessions. And after a time, he start to feel like he was getting to be a clown performing for a drink of rum, sorta like the man they call Henry Gaye who used to go in front of the rumshop every Saturday morning and crow like a cock and wait for somebody to give him a drink of rum or a few shillings. And he couldn't stand these new fellars, these, as he call them, force-ripe, over-night big shots, like Mitchell, loud with their importance because they could afford to buy a bottle, slapping him on the back and saying any foolishness that come in their mouths. Clem say that what really upset him was the joke they was making of stickfighting. He start to be vex with himself for aiding and abetting them because to him, stickfighting was a sacred thing, something for warriors.

'We playing the arse here, you know,' he tell Clem. 'Who the hell is these people? What we doing here with them?'

'You take everything too serious,' Clem tell him. 'What you worrying yourself for? You know these people not better than you. And even if they want to believe that to buy a rum make them important, what you going to do? When I take up my guitar, I don't sing for them, I sing for me; and when you dance in the stickfight ring, you dance for you. They know it.'

'No, they don't know it,' Bolo tell him. 'They believe that to buy a rum is everything. They believe we putting on a show for them.'

'Well, I know it,' Clem say. But then, Clem was like that. He could enter anything and it wouldn't touch him. No matter how he laugh and play the clown, nothing could make him less than himself. Bolo was not like that. He give himself to things.

He was too open to every glance. Things touched him too much. A breeze could cut him.

So now, though Bolo continue to go to Buntin shop on a evening, he buy his own rum and take no further part in the singing and mock stickfighting.

The fellars ask Clem, 'Clem man, what wrong with Bolo? How he not joining in?' for though Bolo stop, Clem continue to sing and play when he feel to.

'Ask him,' Clem tell them.

But they ain't ask Bolo nothing. They see something in his eyes and in how his body set and in the way he sit down that is a warning. Bee see it too. Everybody see this thing in Bolo, except Mitchell. So it will be Mitchell blindness that will make us see a different Bolo.

As they tell it, Clem and Bolo was sitting quiet with a nip of rum there at Buntin when Mitchell come in in his big show-off way, hailing out loud to all, so everybody would know he arrive.

'What happen' here? Is a funeral or what? How it so quiet? Clem, let we get some life in this place. Buntin, bring a bottle for these men.'

'We have rum here,' Clem say.

'You call *this* rum?' And he take up from the table their nip of rum that had some drink in it before it was finish, and laughing, he throw it to one of the loafers who hanging around there.

'Drink it,' he say when the fellar look at Bolo and hesitate. 'Buntin, bring *rum*. Come fellars. Clem, bring out your guitar.'

'I ain't in the mood,' Clem say.

'And you, Bolo? What about you?'

'Buntin, bring a nip for me,' Bolo say.

'Mitchell order a bottle for you already,' Buntin say.

'Buntin, bring a nip for *me*.'

And now Mitchell stand up in front Bolo, 'Bolo, you know what wrong with you,' Mitchell say, his voice big so that the whole place get silent, for the man Mitchell talking to is Bolo. I know the two men, and I know Mitchell could never like Bolo. There is something in Bolo that Mitchell with all his money don't have, a beauty, not of face, Bolo don't have what you would call a pretty face: nose broad, growing like the roots of a mangrove tree from below the high cheekbones of his face, lips curl up like the edge of a cashew fruit – but a spirit, a belonging to the place, a respect that Mitchell feel should be his own because of his prosperity. 'You know what wrong with you? You don't know how to change. You don't know how to use your brains. You sit down here thinking you is king, holding on to your stickfight fame, and don't realise that things ain't the same and the days you waiting on not coming back again. Why you don't do like everybody and have a good time and try to make some money now that the Yankees giving it away on the Base. Look at me . . .'

And Mitchell tell again the story that we hear already: how he come from St John with a saw and hammer and went to the Base and tell them he's a carpenter, spend six months carpentering without driving a nail, and everything he do he use his brains. Mitchell shoulda see that Bolo didn't laugh at the joke Clem say, but no, Mitchell want to rub in his victory, so he say to Bolo, 'Come, take a drink with me. Buntin, bring a bottle. Let's get the place lively. Come.' And with that he put a hand on Bolo shoulder. That is when Bolo hit him, one butt that fling him halfway across the room and send him to the floor, his nose bleeding and one eye shut. Opening his one eye from where he was on the floor, asking, 'What happen, Bolo? What happen?'

After that the men in the rumshop get very careful how they talk to Bolo. Something change in Bolo too. Now, when he walk the village, he didn't have that free easy stride, that smooth fluent joyful walk that we use to so admire. A stiffness come over him. When somebody make a joke with him, his

27

smile was just a stiffening of the face; and in the market, of all of us, only Mother Ruby had the bravery to call out to him, 'Hey, how my husband passing me so straight?' But the rest of us feel afraid to disturb him.

'Clem, tell us, what really happen to him?' we ask, for if anybody to know about Bolo, Clem is the one. Clem feel the same uneasiness with him and though after work on the Estate they would still go and split a nip at Buntin, for both of them it was a strain.

Clem was always a lively fellow and he remain so, singing and making jokes, happy to be among people, especially if they is women, and to let his spirit flow whether he was at a stick-fight or a wake, telling children stories to frighten them, or breaking away from the circle of men ringing bamboo joints on the ground and dancing the bongo, dipping and leaping up like the flames of a flambeau lighting up the ring; and he had the same liveliness in the rumshop with the hustlers or with the soldiers who wanted to hear him sing a calypso.

When everybody rushing to work for the big money on the Base, he was one of the few who remain on the Estate. But even so, he was seeing a new time coming. New times didn't frighten him. Everything had to move on. Things had to change. As he himself say, even he was taking the old music, stickfight tunes, and bongo songs and putting words to them and singing them as calypso. More and more Clem was singing calypso.

One morning Clem get up and he didn't want to stay in Bonasse again. He figured the best thing to do was to go to Port of Spain and try his luck singing calypso. We advise him, 'Go! And see if you could get Bolo to go too. He getting too sour in this place. A change will do him good.'

Bolo had consider leaving the Estate and going to get a job on the American Base. He thought maybe he would like to drive a tractor like one of those that was working on the road the

Americans was cutting through the forest between Bonasse and Charlotte, one of those big ones with the high seat and the long iron hands, that when you pull the lever, the hands go down and close around the earth and lift it up, and when you twist the same lever, the hands swing around and dump the earth in another place; a tractor like that. And, he tell Clem, it had cross his mind to leave Bonasse altogether and try for a job in the oil fields so he could make some money and come back home to Bonasse just to show fellars like Mitchell how to be a man when you have money in your pocket. But in the end he didn't want to leave his mother in Bonasse alone. All her other children was away. So Bolo watch Clem go. We miss Clem too.

Clem went to Port of Spain. We hear from his brother that he get a spot singing in the Old Brigade Calypso Tent. Then we didn't hear about Clem. Years after we would hear Lord Trafalgar singing a song over the radio to a tune we know as bongo.

> *The Yankees came*
> *Oh, what a shame*
> *If you see whores in Port of Spain.*

'Wait, that is Clem,' we say; and in truth it was Clem.

We miss Clem. When he was in Bonasse singing, with all the changes, we had a feeling that the village was still our own. Now he wasn't there we feel more and more that it don't belong to us. And we watch the girls passing in their tight dresses and high heel shoes that they is experts at walking in, making their behinds tremble, or to roll slow, slow like a steam-roller that have the whole year to cross to wherever it have to go: the hustlers practising the steps of the jitterbug on the side of the street, and the Yankee soldiers skidding their jeeps to a stop and jumping over the sides, without bothering to open the doors, the old men moving aside to give them room to pass. This war. This war. In the Anglican and Catholic church, especially, minister and priest was praying for a British victory and people was contributing money to the Red Cross and Salvation Army to help our men fight overseas. The Union Jack was flying in every Bonasse breeze, and in the school where Ivan Morton teach, they had the little children singing,

> Rule Britannia
> Britannia rules the waves
> Britons never never never
> shall be slaves.

In our church where Bee is the leader, we pray for the war to end too, so that the Yankees could go back home and the village could come back to its senses and the girls could come off the streets. Lots of people don't want the war to end. They wish the Yankees and their money stay forever. But to some of us, our life was draining away. Bolo was not happy; still, when somebody die he would go to the wake, and if a man want help on his land or to build a house he would help him. Then sudden, we start to see him in our church. For years his mother is a staunch member, but he was never regular and I wasn't the only one to wonder why. At first we thought that it was Sister Elmilinda daughter, Thelma, who was in Bonasse from Arima to spend time, and for awhile she draw a smile from his, so we think it is she he was coming to see. Then Thelma leave and go back to Arima. Bolo still come to church. And we see it now: Bolo was looking to the church, looking to Bee, as if there is something he expect Bee to do to change what was happening in Bonasse. And truly, there was a time when that was possible, long ago, but now was a different story.

Our church is not like other people own. True, we worship the same Jehovah God, but we in the Spiritual Baptist religion was under steady persecution long before the Americans dream of coming to put up a Base on this island. And even as I, we, was wondering what it is that Bolo expect us to do, more trouble was coming to meet us and why? What we do? Let me tell you.

3 We Church

We have this church in the village. We have this church. The walls make out of mud, the roof covered with carrat leaves: a simple hut with no steeple or cross or acolytes or white priests or latin ceremonies. But is our own. Black people own it. Government ain't spent one cent helping us to build it or to put bench in it or anything; the bell that we ring when we call to the Spirit is our money that pay for it. So we have this church.

We have this church where we gather to sing hymns and ring the bell and shout hallelujah and speak in tongues when the Spirit come; and we carry the Word to the downtrodden and the forgotten and the lame and the beaten, and we touch black people soul.

We never ask nobody to come and join us; but somebody will get a dream, somebody will get a vision, and he come to us and we baptise him in the river and put him out on the Mournin' Ground to pray and fast and wait for the Lord to send him a sign so he will know if his mission is to be a shepherd to the sheep, or a nurse, or a surveyor, or if he call to be a prover to prove out the sheep from the goat and to search out the mockers from the true, or if he is to be a warrior like Bolo.

We ain't do the whiteman or his brown tools any wrong. If a black man want to be a Catholic to kneel down in front of white saints, we don't cry him down. We preach the Word and who have ears to hear, hear. And the lost souls scattered in every religion in Babylon was coming home to a Church that is their own, where after the service finish the brethren could discuss together how the corn growing, how the children doing, for what price cocoa selling, and the men could know which brother they should lend a hand to the coming week, and the sisters could find out who sick from the congregation so we could go and sit with her a little and help her out with the cooking for her children or the washing or the ironing. And it was nice at last to have a place to be together, where you could hear your own voice shouting hallelujah and feel the Spirit spreading over the Church as the brethren sing and dance and catch the power. We was going good – not the best but good enough for a people who bring our bare hands with us from Africa and go through trials and tribulations enough to make a weaker people surrender. But they was watching us.

All of a sudden they start to teach in their schools and in their church that we uncivilized and barbarous. They start telling the little children all kinda lies to scare them away from us – Spiritual Baptist bad, Spiritual Baptist stupid, Spiritual Baptist does deal with the devil, Spiritual Baptist ain't going to heaven. They frighten away the little ones so and draw away from us, especially those who was going to their schools – the bright little ones whose brains they will confuse with their education. And the young men and women, they make these believe that if they give up the church and turn Catholic or Anglican they would not only get a good job but would have a better chance to get to heaven. But even so, enough of us remain. Enough of us remain to sing the hymns and clap hands and make a joyful noise unto the Lord who keep us and strengthen us to reach another day in this tribulation country far away from Africa, the home that we don't know. And black people was still having dreams and visions and coming to us for baptism. So they had to find another plan to make us surrender. And they find it too.

Now everything we do is something wrong. They complain

that we sing too loud, we disturbing the peace. They send six police with a paper to make us move the church from off the main street. We build a new church. They decide that it ain't build strong enough; they make us break it down; and when we try to build another one, they wouldn't okay the plans. So they had us running around – from pillar to post – some of our congregation dropping out on the way, but still we had enough of us to sing the hymns and ring the bell and shout hallelujah when the Spirit come. And black people, Jesus, was still having dreams and seeing visions, and coming to baptise into the religion. On Sundays in those days, we use to welcome brethren from Siparia and Moruga and Sangre Grande for a joint Baptism, and sing? Lord, we would sing those Sunday mornings! The brethren from the church that was visiting would meet us out in the street and we would have a procession with all our members deck out in their best – the nurses in white, the sisters in blue and brown, and our Leader in front with the seals and the shepherd crook and his robe, and we would salute the visiting brethren down the line, pressing our cheeks against theirs, holding their hands in ours and speaking out in tongues, bending our knees to salute the Saviour that would bring together from all parts of the island a tribe of people that was going through the same sufferation. But they have the lawyers. They have the police. They is the Government.

Then one day it was in the papers. They pass the law against us that make it a crime on the whole island for people to worship God in the Spiritual Baptist religion. Now if we ring the bell, that was against the law. If we clap we hands and catch the Spirit, the police could arrest us. One day we was Baptist, the next day we is criminals.

What to do? Who to appeal to? We moved again. We run.

So now the church we have is on the edge of the village, high up on a steep hill, far up in a wilderness place, a little mud hut hiding behind a row of half-dead mango trees. And we have a look-out to watch for the police so if they creep up on us and we don't have time to run we could pretend that we keeping an agriculture meeting. It look to me that this was where they wanted us to be – out of the village. And once they had us in our place, they eased up the pressure a little and forget that we exist, until sudden one night we would hear whistles blowing and the tramp of feet, and we'd bolt through the bush in the night, running like thief, and we would remember what we was forgetting, that we was still illegal, that they could stamp us out any time. Then the war came and find us still here in Bonasse – not all of us who begin the journey, some drop out to join the Adventist, some go and take up with Methodist – but enough to sing the hymns and catch the Spirit and run when the police come. Still, black people was having dreams and visions and coming in secret for baptism. And we was going along, not the best, but we was going along.

You would think that they woulda have their hands full fighting the Japanese, and with the Germans bombing London; but no. That year in all the confusion, with the ban on stickfighting in the village and the gayappe and lend-hand dying and the place groggy with hustlers and American soldiers, that is the year they send Corporal Prince to Bonasse to finish us off.

Plenty corporals pass through Bonasse police station: Standford, Roberts, Lynch, and lately, Busby. All of them had their duty to do, but they know we is not criminals and they use a little reason: they leave us alone once we don't broadcast that we have a Baptist church going on in the village. True, we use to send them, now and then, a bunch of plantains or some pigeon peas, and Corporal Busby use to get his regular chicken because he use to tip us off about the days they was going to raid the church. They was police, but they was human too. Corporal Prince was a different story.

Tall, stocky as a gru-gru tree, this policeman show no sympathy or respect or mercy for people black like he. He was the law. The whiteman send him to do a job, and he do it, like a tank or a tractor or an elephant gone mad, bowling over and uprooting and smashing without human compassion or reasoning; and where another policeman mighta hesitate to smash up a church his father and grandfather worship in, Prince had no sense of danger or remembrance or love or fear. The law was all that concerned him; and it was a sweetness for him to mash up your face or break down your church if you is Baptist. The week before they send him to Bonasse, he was in Jericho where he arrest Pastor Maynard, the leader of the church there, and cuff down with his own fist Pastor Maynard son, the one call Ruben, when the boy try to hold on to the baton he (Prince) was bringing down on his father head. The week before that, he and five constables went over to Charlotte and break into Leader Samuel church while the brethren was praying and beat the congregation and mash up the benches and seize the bell they was ringing as evidence to show that they is criminals, then they turn around and arrest ten of the oldest who couldn't run or who refused to run from them.

This man is in Bonasse now, walking down the main street, big, black, powerful and slow, with his hammer head sticking out the back of his blue police cap, his size thirteen police boots hitting the ground, brap! brap! brap! and his shoulders crouched over and his long hands hanging down his sides like a wrestler, as if he don't really care to use the brown baton peeping out his trousers pocket, prefer to handle any trouble, strangle any man with his bare hands.

So we gather now, the few of us who come through the trial and tribulation years together, in our yard in front the house that Bee build, first for him and me and then for our one, two, three, four, five children, on this evening with the sky red below the blue where the sun going down behind the sea and the darkness creeping up between the coconut trees and all the greeness getting grey, and in the mango tree in the yard a blue bird too young to fly, hopping from limb to limb, calling out in its infant voice, cheep! cheep! and making a pause to listen for the mother to answer and no answer. We sit down in the last light of the evening on the front steps and the two bench that I take out from the kitchen. And Bee talk, giving us the history of the trials and tribulations we go through in this Babylon country, where no matter what we do to be ourselves they try to make us illegal, to cut us off from our God and self and leave us naked without defence.

And the night was falling, and from below the coconut trees I could hear the cigales bawling, and the young blue bird in the mango tree, tired from crying for his mother all evening, was making longer pauses in his cheeping and still no answer from the darkness. And Bee was saying in a voice full up with all the years of sufferation and the trying and not knowing what tomorrow will bring and knowing that we have children and the police have guns and we have to try and try to find a way, Bee was saying that we have to find some way to survive for Prince come to Bonasse with one intention: to mash up the church and get promotion, and he will knock down his own mother if she stand in his way.

And before Bee words was well out his mouth, Bolo was saying, as if his own words was there in his bowels waiting, 'We have to kill Prince.' Saying it without vexation or hesitation or excitement or fear, calm, certain like a judge, the words booming out of his belly, his guts. 'We have to kill him!' Kill him. Kill him. And everybody get silent, listening again to hear what we already heard: we have to kill him. And in my ears, the words, Bolo words ringing like a church bell still tingling after it finish ring. And the men sit down with their eyes looking straight in front of them, and none of them breathing, and I, we, waiting to hear their answer. And Bolo there stand up straight, tall as a young balata tree, with his head turn to the sky and the smoke from his cigarette climbing slow, making a net above his head, and the silence stretching, steretching, stretching, until Brother Oswald break it.

'We will have to talk to the authorities,' Brother Oswald say. 'Protest. Let them know that we is British citizens too. Let them know that is advantage they taking on black people.'

And Bolo stand up stiffer and his head more straight. And all of us waiting, and Oswald words still there.

'Brethren,' Brother Oswald say. 'We have to get a man they will listen to, a man who they respect and who could talk for us.' Nobody say nothing.

In a woman's way, I could understand why these men don't know what to say. I know as well as they that we talk to the authorities already and that that ain't solve nothing and the main thing to do should be . . . I wouldn't say kill. No, not kill Prince, but at least do something to make him feel, to hurt him, so that he and those who send him will know that we ain't prepare to give up without a struggle. But I know this is not a easy thing for them to decide to do. And I don't mean that they not brave. The men have to think about more than their bravery. They have to think about the church and how it going to live. They have to think about our children who we want to see grow big. Because once you start against the police, you have to continue. So I know is something they have to give proper consideration to; but even so, I agree with Sister Ruth when she say, 'But we talk to them already, and they never listen. What they want us to do?'

'That is why we have to get a man they will listen to,' Brother Oswald say. 'A man with voice.' And now all eyes turn to Bee.

'Brother Bolo,' Bee say, 'we is people. The police have to respect us.'

'Yes,' Oswald say.

'Brother Bolo, if we break the law, let them take us to court.

We not animals for them to beat. We not criminals to run from police.'

'Yes,' Oswald say. 'Yes.'

'Brothers and sisters,' Oswald say, beginning his own plea, but Bee lift up his hands and stop him.

'Brothers and Sisters,' Bee say, 'I know we talk and plead with them already. I know they treat us like beast, but to kill a policeman is to set yourself on a road of no returning. And we have children. And we have the church to keep alive. I say we have to find another way.'

'Look,' Brother Oswald say, happy now after Bee speak, 'we have right here in the village a man who could advise us what to do. Why we don't talk to him before we do anything?'

'Who?' Bee ask. But nobody had to answer, all of us know the man is Ivan Morton.

Is so Ivan Morton come into this story, though you could say he was in it already; born in it right here in Bonasse in a little wood house his father, Fitzie Morton, put up at the end of the trace next to the Estate and spend his whole life extending, adding one room to another with years between them, without no chart or plan other than to get more space to put the children that his wife keep making every Monday morning; and he never finish it. Never finish it, fall off a coconut tree he was climbing on the Estate where he make his living, break a hand, a foot, his hip and some ribs, and stay laid up for eighteen months without getting a cent compensation from Mr Richardson though he work on the Estate from since he was eleven. So that his wife, Miss Maude, Ivan mother, had to take in washing from the same Mr Richardson to keep the house together and the children in school – though by that time some of them was big enough to manage for theyself. Fitzroy, the biggest boy, went to stay with a relative in San Fernando, and later we hear that he stow away to Panama, and Irene, the girl after him, went to Port of Spain to be a nurse, though people say she find a different occupation in the city, but the truth is nobody ever see her again. Ivan was the lucky one. He was the youngest and he had the brains. So he was in it from small, seeing his father sitting on the verandah of his unfinish house with his foot stretch out, his chest strap down and his hand in a sling, staring out at the Estate and the wicked coconut trees he would never climb again and at Mr Richardson big house on the hill looking over the village, cursing his bad luck, Mr Richardson and God, there in it to see his mother every day over the tub, washing, washing, until she begin to resemble a scrubbed out scrubbing board, but with all that, boasting to my mother that he wouldn't miss a day school even if she have to wash his one khaki pants on Fridays and put his blue shirt in the tub every other evening. And all she had was this hope, this faith that he would learn his lessons and pass his examination and come to be in a position to bear better than she and Mr Fitzie and his brothers and sisters before him, the burden all black people call upon to bear, or better still, make the miracle, qualify himself and rise to take up the greater burden to lead his people out of the hands of Pharaoh.

Ivan didn't let her down. A small, thin foot little boy with big dreaming eyes popping out his face, a serious quiet child with no interest in spinning top or flying kite or pitching marbles, he was first in all his classes in Bonasse R.C. School, and by the time he was eleven, he make the first miracle. He was in Exhibition class, ready to sit the college exhibition examination which, if he pass, would give him the chance of going away to Port of Spain to St Mary's or Queen's Royal College.

I myself was a young lady in that time, but I remember that from young he belong not just to Miss Maude and Mr Fitzie, but was the hope of the whole village. And while we was praying for him and Mr Headly was giving him private lessons to sharpen him up, at home his mother, Miss Maude, was doing her best to feed him well, to give him the extra egg, the fish-head soup, the cod liver oil, the drops of phosphorene to strengthen his brain to take in the lessons he had to take in if he was going to win one of the four college exhibitions. And when she come to church – our church, for she was a Baptist in those days – Miss Maude would get down on her knees, and we would go down too and pray with her for God to smile on the boy and bring a brightness in his way and open his brains like Solomon, to wisdom, knowledge and understanding. He himself; didn't come to church often 'cause he had to learn his lessons, so I guess he didn't know how much prayers we say for him; and when he pass us in the street, his chin up, scenting another air and his gaze far away as if he wasn't here in Bonasse, not seeing the place or the people, we nod our heads and smile: we understand. We understand that a boy with all that brain and that great burden on him at such a early age, wouldn't have time to see people. Still he was our own boy. The day he was going to San Fernando to sit the exam, all the neighbours living near gather in the morning with the rising sun and make a procession right down to the bus station, with him in the centre, his eyes wide and frighten, his thin legs shining with coconut oil, his socks pull up to his knobbly knees, holding to his chest a bottle of ink and a ruler, marching like a tired soldier in the new brown shoes he was wearing for the first time.

So he was in it and sit the college Exhibition examination and fail it – two times – not, his mother say afterwards, because he wasn't bright but because he wasn't Catholic or Anglican. Was to imagine the commotion that evening when Mr Headly come with the news that Ivan fail the exam again. Miss Maude, washing in the yard, give out one big scream and faint away and all the neighbours – all of us, my mother and Miss Jordan and old Tantie Laurie – had to rush out and hold her up and rub her hands and face with soursop leaves and lift up and

41

carry her inside and bawl and mourn and console with her at the wickedness of the authorities. Mr Fitzie was not at home, he was back working on Richardson Estate, not climbing coconut trees again but driving the donkey cart now, a boy with him, gathering nuts that fall off the Estate trees. The fall make him a disgruntled man, stiff and bitter, walking with a limp from his broken hip and always smelling of rum from the nip in his back pocket. Nobody know how much he care about Ivan and his education, but when he come home and get the news that his son didn't pass, he strap his poniard case around his waist and put his sharpen cutlass in it and was ready with tears in his eyes to take the little money that he had and catch a taxi to Port of Spain and seek out the jackass who say that his son who was coming first in every test he sit in Bonasse Roman Catholic School couldn't win a college exhibition. The men had to hold him down. He fight them. They hold him down. And he didn't stop struggling until Uncle Cornelius (who know about these things) tell him that the examination papers does correct in England.

Now what for Ivan to do? College is out of the queston, Miss Maude and Mr Fitzie ain't had the money to pay even if the schools accept him. And then they realise that his education ain't prepare him for nothing. He couldn't go and work on the Estate which is the only work for people to do. The only thing was for him to try to be a pupil teacher in the Catholic school. So he went to the priest. Okay, the priest tell him, for the priest know how good he was in school. The only thing is that to teach in the Catholic school you have to be Catholic. What to do? We have no Baptist school for him to teach in. We have no college to send him to. What for him to do?

'Turn Catholic,' his mother tell him. 'Maybe things will get better for you.' Miss Maude, his mother, turn Catholic too, and for a time she stop talking to all the neighbours, but my mother had better sense than to vex with her. 'Miss Maude,'

Ma tell her, 'you do what you have to do. We don't hold it against you. We say a lot of prayers for Ivan in the Baptist church and we ain't see them come through.' But though she get back friendly with us, a coolness remain, a kinda suspicion and shame.

So Ivan Morton turn Catholic and learn their catechism and went to confession and make his first communion. But he was still our own boy, and when he went to the Teachers Training College in Port of Spain and pass his examination there, we buy a newspaper just to see his name.

Now he is a man and the whole village know his name, for he is a full-fledge teacher in Bonasse R.C. School. Parents go to him and talk 'bout how their children doing and to tell him not to 'fraid to straighten them out with a good flogging. In the village people respect him, and if we have a function to give, a son to marry, a child to christen, we want him at the ceremony to give a toast, to say the words that will bring a kind of decoration to the occasion. The warden and the sergeant of police and the magistrate respect him too and he is one man not frighten to stand up and talk to Mr Richardson. This is the man. So is no surprise that is he that Brother Oswald have in mind to talk for us.

But Bolo don't intend to give up his manness without a struggle.

'Ivan Morton?' he ask. 'You sure Ivan Morton is the man to talk for you?'

There is a reason why Bolo ask that question. To understand it we have to go back a little to that year when Bolo was nineteen. He wasn't champion yet, and wouldn't be for a year or two; but in the stickfights of that year, he had beat Zephryn from Mayaro and fight to a draw in the battle with Big Brother at Valencia, and at the fight in Moruga, Dido, the Moruga Phantom, hug him up and hold up his hands and say for everybody to hear, 'This boy is a champion.' That was after he block

Dido best shots and was still there in the gayelle, weaving and dancing and sliding in on Dido, and Dido don't know what to do. When they came back from Moruga, the men of the village put him up on their shoulder and parade him down Main Street. So that year when he was nineteen, though he wasn't yet champion, the whole village know that after King Riley, the next king to reign in Bonasse is Bolo. So he was already a prince in the village, drinking with the true stickfighters, fellows calling out to him to be in his company and all the girls' eyes on him.

So there in the village is Bolo, slim, tall, good-looking, the fastest and the strongest and the bravest young man in Bonasse, a young tiger, the uncrowned king. There is Bolo, his hips narrow, his chest broad, walking with that racehorse brisk, quick-stepping prancing with his spirit rearing up inside of him, walking with a kind of stuttering speed as if is a struggle to hold back his feet from running away with him. And here is this girl, Eulalie Clifford from River Road, belle of the village, a young filly frisking her tail, moving with that smooth, soft teasing womanness, with her eyes bold and down-looking and smiling and though her dress make out of the same material they use to make dresses for any girl, Eulalie Clifford dress have a kind of spring in it, a kinda thing, a life in it that when she walk, her skirt hit her hips and the cloth dance up and hold onto her body and strain against her flesh as if is not cloth at all but a living thing. Here is this girl, brisk, bright-eyed, her black smooth-skin body carrying a warm woman aliveness and rhythm of joy, swinging across the unpave roads, watering the mouths of every male that see her and making the old women smile and nod their heads and want to reach out and touch her with their hands to bless her.

Everybody know it. The young men know it, and the young girls know it: the girl to get Bolo is Eulalie, and if any young man is to keep Eulalie still long enough to put a ring on her finger, is Bolo. The two of them know it too, so they ain't in no hurry. Like two stickfighters in the same small ring, they move through the village like they not seeing each other, but we know that both of them circling, dancing to the drums and the singing, showing off their aliveness and beauty: they have time, for to meet they will meet.

Then in the Easter of that year, Ivan Morton come back home on vacation from the Teachers Training College in Port of Spain where he was spending two years. His father was dead already, mcst of his brothers gone away, but his mother still there in the house, a tired, scrubbed-out old lady with not too many years to see again. He come to the village with his tie on and his hair part on the left side, his shoes shining, and his pen clip to his shirt pocket. And he young, but not in the same way that Bolo and the other village young men young. He young in a older, more settled way, polished, you could say, like if the village get too small for him, like if he spread open his hands he could touch the sides of the village. He see Eulalie and his eyes catch fire, and Eulalie can't help but see him, for he stand out in Bonasse, and though he didn't pass his final exam yet, we have pride in him. He is our own boy.

Nobody know what make Eulalie choose Ivan Morton above Bolo, if that is what she really do, if that is what really happen. Some say is the fountain pen she see clip onto his shirt pocket, some say that he talk and impress her with his English; that she was never really serious about Ivan, that what she wanted to do was to test Bolo to see if he would fight for her. I don't know. What we see that Easter in the village is Eulalie and Ivan strolling down the beach. What we see is Eulalie walking with her hummingbird briskness tamed down, her two eyes on Ivan Morton face. We have every year in Bonasse a big harvest dance with a band from San Fernando and people coming from all over the island. That is where you see between the boys and girls who like who. Well, after the dance, it was Ivan Morton who walk Eulalie home past the cemetery and the big bridge to River Road where she live.

Then a few months after Ivan leave and gone back to Port of Spain, Eulalie Clifford wasn't swinging her hips again, because hips don't swing too easy when a girl in the family way. So she had the baby. We was expecting Ivan to put ring on her finger, if not immediate, at least after he finish with his examination, but that magic didn't happen.

Poor Eulalie. Some say she was a fool to throw 'way her chances with Bolo, who she know, and go with Ivan Morton. But when I look at it, I see that what happen with Eulalie was showing something bigger that was happening in the village right under our nose. What was happening was that the warrior was dying in the village as the chief figure. The scholar, the boy with education, was taking over and if we was thinking, we wouldn't be surprised for now education was getting popular as the way to win the battle to be somebody; and the warriors, the men to fight real fights, was just something to remember, for they never win no battle and if they do anything, is to bring us more trouble. We shoulda take more notice of what happen with Eulalie. Poor Eulalie. Ivan Morton leave her with the baby and take up a light-skin girl from Tunapuna, married her and bring her with him from the Training College to live in Bonasse. Some of us grumble a little, but that was all; but to the majority, Eulalie look for her own trouble. So that is how this evening, with night nearly upon us, and ten years later and we in this big trouble, Bolo could ask the question, if we sure that Ivan Morton is the man to talk for us.

A leader is a man with a heavy weight on his shoulders. Is not for himself alone he acting, but for everybody, and even if Bee want to deal with his own manness (and I not saying he not frighten too), his is the voice to speak not for himself alone, but for the people, and for us; is fifty/fifty between killing Prince and talking to Ivan Morton. Bee job is to keep the church alive.

So Bee say that, yes, he will go and talk to Ivan Morton.

'We have to change the law first,' Bee say when he come back from seeing Ivan Morton. 'We have to put a man of our own in the Legislative Council to speak for us, to make the law protect us as the law is suppose to and to keep the police from brutalising our people.'

'This is what you get from Ivan Morton?' Bolo ask. 'When all this will happen? Right now we don't have land and property, so we can't vote. When all this will happen?'

'Soon as the war over, Brother Bolo,' Bee say. 'Britain will have to give us the vote. One man one vote.'

'And what we going to do now? Run again?' Bolo ask.

'Well,' said Brother Oswald, bowing his head and sighing as a man who was ready to take up a familiar burden before he set out again, 'we accustom running. I guess we could run again. Is not for long.'

'You ain't tired running?' Bolo ask. 'You ain't tired? Kill Prince!'

'And when they send another policeman, kill him too? You will kill the whole Police Force, Brother Bolo?' Brother Sylvester ask.

'Brethren,' Bee say, 'when your hand is in the lion mouth, you have to ease it out. We have to be wise as the serpent and harmless as the dove. We . . .'

'Don't count on me!' Bolo say. 'I is no dove for them to brutalise me.'

'Brethren,' Bee say, 'if a man compel you to walk one mile with him, go two; if he ask you for your cloak, give him your coat too. We going to do what they want us to do. We going to try it their way. They want us to not ring the bell, we not going to ring the bell. They want us to be Anglican and Catholic, we going to be like Catholic and Anglican. We going to sing how they want us to sing, we going to pray quiet just as they pray. We going to worship like them. The war can't go on forever.

47

We going to get the vote and elect our own man to the Council, then we going to be free, free to worship, free to sing.'

'Hallelujah!' Sister Fanny cry out.

'Amen!' say Brother Remy.

But on Bolo face and in his eyes and how his jaw bulge, his vexation was plain as day.

I thought that we woulda never see him in the church again, that he would go away, forget us, but he was there next Sunday, sitting alone in the last bench, holding himself tall and apart from us, not so much in vexation as with a waiting kind of knowing patience, as if he expect us to see our mistake and turn from it before is too late.

So now we have this church on top of this hill on the edge of the village. We have this church, where Bee preach the sermons quiet, without spirit so as not to move the congregation to sing too loud or ring the bell or catch the Spirit and speak in tongues, so when Corporal Prince break into the church one evening, he and the whole Bonasse Police Force, he find us singing soft and low as children in Sunday school: 'God moves in mysterious way His wonders to perform.' We wasn't breaking the law, so they had was to put up their batons and go away without beating anybody . . . And so we go.

But the more we go on with this type of service, this soft praying and quiet singing, and not ringing the bell or catching the Spirit, the more we realize that we ain't solving the problem. All we was doing was taking away the ceremonies natural to our worship. All we was doing was watering down the beauty and appeal of our church. And what we was becoming? What was we becoming?

And Bolo is there in the church with his tall, serious, silent watching self, waiting; and Bee can't look at him – though more and more Bee can't look at anybody – for the war is not ending, Britain ain't thinking of black people voting, and instead of the church improving, more and more people was going away – not that you could blame them – for people don't stay in a religion because is a fashion, but because it offer their spirit something. And what this kinda church we now had was offering? For us to be in the same place at the same time to watch one another face and cry inside to see how weak we come, to see how we can't shout or ring the bell and have to stifle hallelujah in our throat? And if people had visions that send them to us for baptism, we can't take the chance and baptise them in the river, we can't put them out on Mournin' Ground, because the police have their spies on us, and Prince like a mappipire in the grass waiting. That year we had to send away Miss Grant and Sam Farrell when they come for baptism, and we couldn't baptise Samuel John who travel across half the island to find us. Oh, that year we was going to nothing.

Even our children was getting tired of the watery kind of service our church was offering, and on Sundays, the bigger ones, Taffy and Winston, instead of coming with us to church, would sneak off to play cricket on the savannah or to catch fish down the bay. And what Bee could tell them? What Bee could say?

And every Sunday Bolo is there in church, tall, unbending, his face stiff, his eyes burning. He not singing the hymns; he not praying. He is just there like a hard question staring in everybody face. The men try to look at him. They try, but as his eyes move to hold theirs, they turn from his face. Every Sunday he in church. And now is in their eyes: if they have to pick between killing Prince and killing Bolo, I not so sure Bolo would be alive another day. Bolo know this too, but he back in church next Sunday to face it and to make them face again the question that he is representing. And Bee, getting tired of waiting on the war to end, turn and look again to Ivan Morton.

Every Sunday morning Ivan Morton pass in front our house on the way to the Catholic church, he and his wife, the starched, tall, light-skin lady from St Joseph, so frail that a

49

breeze could blow away. Every Sunday morning just when the Catholic church bell tolling, we see them: he with his jacket and tie, walking slow to keep from perspiring in the hot bright morning, she with her rosary and prayer book and her white veil falling over the stiff black curls on her pressed hair, her two careful knees barely bothering the cloth of her dress hanging down to her ankles. If it was Eulalie walking by the side of Ivan Morton, her chest woulda been jumping and her bodyline rolling to make that white dress dance and sing and the grass stand up and coconut trees bend down to say good morning. But I guess a school teacher need a wife who not going to make a mistake with her English. Every Sunday they go. And Bee sit down on the front steps with his body bend over and his chin pressing down on his two hands ball into two fists, watching Ivan Morton pass, waiting for a sign, something from him; and Ivan Morton waves, and his wife smiles and say her nice good morning and they go their way leaving their cologne trailing behind them for us to smell. Every Sunday morning Bee take his hand from under his chin and wave to them.

Then one Sunday morning – the Mortons had just pass and gone their way – Bee come into the kitchen where I kneading flour to make a bake.

'I going to break the law, Eva,' he say.

He was behind me. I didn't turn around to look at him. 'You going to break the law?' I ask him. Because I know the law don't make fun. I know that when the whiteman write down something, it well write down. 'You going to break the law?'

'I going to break it,' he say.

4 To Break the Law

And now, every evening when Bee come back from grazing the heifer, he stand up on the front steps and watch the darkness coming on and the birds flying to nest and say with the same newness as if he never say it before, 'I going to break this law.'

I could understand how Bee, tired of waiting for this war to end, feeling he must give a answer to Bolo, wanting in a man-way to rise to the man-challenge in front of him, not to mention wanting to keep a hold on the congregation that daily dwindling away. I could understand how Bee would want to break the law . . . but talking ain't making it break, and we have children. The children hearing him. And they not thinking about the trouble it going to bring, they waiting to see him break the law in truth.

We have five children. Winston and Taffy is nearly men, and Joyce is fifteen; and is bad enough for these, the bigger ones, to listen to their father talking and he ain't doing nothing. For after they hear him long enough, they begin to treat what he say as a joke and don't expect nothing from him. I see something breaking between Bee and these children. Still, I know their own life in front of them, and I expect that time would give them the understanding to look back at their father and realize that he wasn't talking just because he want to make a fool of himself, but because in his own way, he was battling to be a man. But we have two other children: Gem is four, a little girl, but a woman still, born with the gift to understand men and so full up with the miracle of her own aliveness, she marvelling to be in a world with moving things and is more interested in climbing on her father lap and watching him cut the grass than in what he saying; but Reggie is a boy-child, eight years old, just at that time in his life when he looking for a father in his father, and what he seeing is this man mumbling how he going to break the law and the law still there.

What to do? I could talk to the child, tell him about the histories we go through, and how the law strong and the police wicked and we few, and how is not every time that a man could do the things that he say he going to do. But how to do that? How to let a boy-child know as soon as his eyes open to the world that we ain't have no power. No. I can't do that to my own child. I can't cripple him before he start to walk. I have to let him see his father as warrior.

'Your father is going to break the law just as he say,' I tell him, 'just wait a little.' And all the time I pray for the miracle to happen.

But no miracle happen. Every Sunday I watch Bee go to the pulpit and open the Bible and my heart would tremble a little, and Reggie would glance at me, and I would listen to Bee preach the sermon without no fire and I would join in the singing of the hymns that was every Sunday getting shorter, and I would die again and die again for Bee, and when I turn I would see Brother Bolo with his stern face watching.

Taffy is the second one, the one after Winston. He go to school and ain't taking schooling: play marbles, spin top, fly kite, and every Friday evening when school breaks out for the weekend he in a fight. The teachers don't know what to do with him again. They sick of talking and they tired of beating him. So I take him outa school and send him by Mr Moses to learn tailoring so that at least he wouldn't have to face the world like his brother, Winston, who ain't know to do nothing except labouring. Taffy have sixteen years. Of all my children he is the one that give me the most trouble to bring into this world, and the way it looking, he going to be the one to send me to my grave quick. Because Taffy have this knife that he grind down from a hacksaw blade and put a handle to, that he always throwing, sticking on the door, in trees, in anything. He have this knife and he have this way about him, this attitude, this gam, this thing in him that the world does beat out of a man before he reach eighteen years, but that ain't beat out of Taffy yet, and is going to be hell to beat out of him. And though I glad to see that the boy have some spirit in him, I does get frighten, I know this country. I know I ain't have money to pay for the trouble he will get himself in – just for the way he does walk and look at people.

I talk to Taffy. Instead Taffy stay in the tailor shop and learn what Moses have to teach him, the boy take up with Sam Wills' sons, a worthless gang of boys that roam the place, looking for fight, cutting with knife, smoking cigarettes, drinking rum and cussing bad words like the Yankee soldiers from the Base.

'Boy,' I tell him, 'you ain't find life too hard with us already for you to be getting yourself in this stupidness? You ain't seeing what going on?'

What Taffy want to do is leave Bonasse and go away.

'Go where? Do what? Be a knife-man? A badjohn?'

Taffy have this other thing in him, this kinda smile and look and voice all in one that no matter how vex I is he could look at me and melt me down like he's the sun and I is butter.

'Ma, what a nice boy like me want to be a badjohn for?' And he smooth his hand over his hair that he spend hours brushing till he get waves to lie down in it. 'I want to go away. See the world. Get a work on a boat, travel. New York, London, Paris, Hong Kong. See snow, wear a winter coat. You don't think I will look nice in a winter coat, Ma?'

53

'Boy, this world ain't making no joke with black people. You have to be able to do something to help yourself if you want to get any place. Why you don't just learn Mr Moses tailoring and try and come out something instead of dreaming nonsense and doing foolishness to get yourself in trouble and me and your father in expense?'

'Ma, Mr Moses too ugly.' (I tell you this boy, Taffy, shoulda be a comic.) 'You never notice how you does get ugly when you stay 'round ugly people?' And he touch his precious hair again. 'Right now I ain't so ugly, but give me one more year with Moses. Give me a year and you wouldn't recognize your own son. Ma, you yourself will cry for me. I will get so black, my hair will get bad, my nose done so big already, will spread across my face and my nose holes will open like Moses own. But if I go . . . . You notice how fellars who travel does look clean and smooth and fair when they come back from away. Port of Spain, Ma! Let me go to Port of Spain, I will stay by Uncle Harvey. I will get a boat to work on there, Bonasse ain't have nothing in it for me.'

'Boy, you too hurry,' I tell him. 'This world not running away.'

One Sunday, I turn around and didn't see Brother Bolo. And now that he was not there in church, he was there more than ever, stronger a question bawling out for a answer. And Bee, getting more weary every day, is still saying that he will break the law, saying the words over and over like a prayer, like a magic chant that if he say long enough will come true by itself. And Reggie is looking at his father. I feel sorry for Reggie but, believe me, I feel more sorry for Bee; and although I know for us it mean trouble, Oh Lord, I wish . . . I wish that Bee would just get up like a wind and break the law and let what happen happen.

Winston want to leave home too. And what Winston want to do? He want to be a policeman.

'A policeman?' I ask him. And I don't mean to blaspheme, but I wonder about life. I wonder if there is not some wickedness set aside for you to meet that you can't escape. I wonder.

'Winston, boy, when you's a police you does have to swear to lock up your mother,' Taffy tell him, in his comic way. 'Boy, the uniform they give you to wear is *dark* blue, and you so black already, people wouldn't make out is you. And in the hot sun, sweat go be running down your face. You go to spend your whole salary on handkerchief.'

Yet, with all his talk, I don't believe that Winston was really serious. I couldn't believe it. And then I see him talking to Bee.

It was evening. I in the front room ironing. Bee sit down on the rocking chair with his head looking up from the Bible he was reading, and Reggie on a stool by the kerosene lamp, doing his home lessons on his lap because I was using the table, and Taffy in a corner at the window where he look out and wait for his friends to pass and whistle him. And there is Winston, a young man, taller now than is father, stand up in the middle of the room, with his two feet near together and don't know what to do with his hands, telling his father that he want to go and sit the police examination. And Bee, letting the Bible go and gripping the arms of the chair with his two hands, and his eyes watching Winston, watching Winston, and Winston uneasy there looking at his father, waiting for Bee to say something.

'Go,' Bee say, very soft. And the boy there with his tall uneasiness. 'Go. You have nineteen years. I can't hold you here. Go!' Bee say, his voice low, stifling.

And Bee remain sitting down with his two hands gripping the chair, with his chin push out, his shoulders steady and his stiff neck straight, as if Winston had strike him a blow that he still had enough strength to take.

'Go!' he say again, his voice rising and breaking as his vexation get the upper hand of him. And Winston stand up in front of him, wanting to move and don't know how to move.

'Go!' And before Winston could do anything, Bee turn to Taffy, 'And you? You don't want to go too? You don't want to be a police too to arrest your own people? You don't want to be one too?'

The children look to me to say something, but I didn't tell Bee anything that time, not there in front of the children. I didn't say a word to him until the next day. After the last two children eat lunch and go back to school, I walk the mile and a half along the trace to the garden where Bee work seven of the toughest acres of land in creation, that by some miracle of faith and patience and plowing and pleading, the earth bring forth plantains and sweet potatoes and ochroes and yams, enough for us to eat a little and to sell some in the market to get money to keep us going.

I go and find him there in the hot sun, in front of the rows and rows of turn up hills of earth he plow that day, standing there with his back wet down with perspiration, lifting up the iron fork in the air and bringing it down and burying it in the earth and turning over the earth and lifting up the fork again, sinking it into the earth with his strength as if it was the earth that hurt him and he wanted to stab it, stab it, stab it until he kill it. I sit down there in the mango tree shade and watch him strain with the fork in the earth, and all around, the black birds on the bushes watching him with his neck muscles swelling and his arms going in that hard rhythm of digging and uprooting, and what I see is a man alone in front all this hard, red earth – and Winston going to be a policeman, and Bolo gone from the church, and Ivan Morton ain't doing nothing, and Reggie watching, and Prince the policeman waiting.

I sit down and watch him drive the fork into the ground, making no grunt, no groan, and his silence is its own cry, shout in the wilderness with the wind around him swaying the bushes and the black birds watching the earthworms crawling out of the ground. I watch him, his digging slowing down, and

I wonder if all this digging and uprooting and sweating and grunting going to bring forth anything, or if all a man could do is dig and uproot and bury seeds in the earth and pray and hope things grow. Then, he sink the fork into the ground and turn to me and sit down by my side.

'Water?' I ask him.

He take the bottle of water from my hand, bend back his head, throw the water in his mouth, spit out the first mouthful, then take a sip, and take a sip again.

'I bring some lemonade for you too.'

But he don't want it. He sit down there facing the land, watching the black birds now hopping over the forked-up earth, tugging worms from the ground.

I turn to him again, 'You want to eat now?'

He shake his head, and shake his head again slow, weary, as if he trying to shake out something sticking in his brain.

'You can't blame the boy, Bee,' I say. 'Is not wickedness that make him want to go away, you know. What we have here to keep him?'

Bee turn his eyes on me.

'Sure you trying with the church, Bee, but look how things going. Every day more people leaving.'

'He is the oldest,' Bee say. 'The one to take over after me.'

'But, take over what? Take what over, Bee?' I say. 'Eh Bee?'

'Children have responsibility,' Bee say.

'And what you asking the boy to be responsible for? A half-dead church where we can't sing or catch the Spirit? What you want the boy to do, Bee?'

'Nothing,' Bee say, 'he ain't responsible for nothing. This land is nothing, and the church don't count. You right, Eva. We don't have nothing to keep him here. Let him go and be a police. Let all of them go. Let them go. I don't know what the hell I killing myself here for.'

'Bee!' And I look at Bee sit down there with his hands

holding his knees together and I see the pain and weariness on his face, and I look across at the iron fork standing where he plant it in the ground . . . 'You have three sons, Bee, one will stay,' I say. 'Soon the war going to end and the Americans going to go away and, as Ivan Morton say, we going to get our own man in the Council.'

'The war will end?' Bee ask. 'The war will end? The war will end but war will never end till people free.' And as if a sudden wisdom hit him, he turn to me, 'Eva, I going to break this law.'

'Yes, Bee,' I say.

And so this Sunday the few of us walk up Zion hill to the church out in the wilderness place, far from the eyes and ears of the police. We stand up and sing the first hymn that as usual don't move nobody. Then Brother Oswald, his big, sad eyes moving restless over the Bible, read the first lesson, the words coming out his mouth in a rush as if he was doing a duty that he in a hurry to finish. He sit down, and we get up and sing another hymn that have no spirit and don't cause us to ring the bell or shout hallelujah or anything, and Taffy by my side start nodding and I elbow him in his ribs for now his father was going to the pulpit, and Reggie turn from me to his father; and the wind was blowing, and though it didn't look like rain was going to fall that day, all of a sudden through the noise of the wind we heard the raindrops pelting, and woosh, the rain began. The church was leaking so the congregation start to move to seats where the water wasn't dripping in through the roofing. On the pulpit Bee wait for us to settle down, then he open the Bible in front of him, bend down his head and start reading:

> 'My people hath been lost sheep,
> Their shepherds have caused them to
> go astray. They have turned them
> away on the mountains. They have

gone from mountain to hill. They
have forgotten their resting place.'

And Bee raise his head from his reading and look at the few of us packed close together in one corner where the building wasn't leaking, and his voice was low and the rain was soft, beating on the roofing, and we was quiet and listening.

'Brethren, tonight I come to bow my head and to lift up my head,' Bee say and right away his words touch me and my mouth answer, 'Blessed!'

'I come tonight,' Bee say, 'to make a confession and to give a direction.'

And Sister Ruth cry out, 'Sweet Jesus!' and raise the hair on my head.

'I come tonight,' Bee say, 'as a man who stumble in the wilderness for nights, and my eyes open now. I see the light! I see the light!' Bee cry out. 'I see the light!'

'Amen,' the congregation say.

'Brethren,' Bee say, his voice soft now and sorrowful and brave and pleading, 'I is the shepherd that cause the sheep to go astray.'

'... astray...' And we was answering him, leading him on, drawing out his words with our own as in the old way.

'... that have you moving from mountain to hill, so we don't know...'

'Jesus, we don't know,' the congregation say.

'I mean,' Bee say, 'we don't know if we is fowl...'

'Say it, Leader.'

'... or feather. If...'

'Merciful Father.'

'... we black...'

'Jeesus!'

'... or white. If...'

'Oh Lord!'

' . . . we going . . .'

'Going, Saviour, going.'

' . . . or coming. If we up . . .'

'Jehovah!'

' . . . or down. We don't know who we is.'

'Tell us, Leader. Tell us who is we.'

'We,' Bee say, ' . . . we is Shadrack, Meshack and Abednigo that burn in the fiery furnace and ain't come out yet . . .'

'Tell it!'

'We is the day that don't have no rest . . .'

'Saviour!'

'We is the grass that they cut and trample and dig out and sprout roots again . . .'

'Beloved!'

'We is sticks that bend and don't break. We is Egypt . . .'

'Oh Jesus!'

'Ethiopia . . .'

'Lord!'

'We is Judah . . .'

'Oh Israel!'

' . . . Solomon, the Queen of Sheba. We is love that rise up, the earth that don't fall down. We is corn and water.'

'Amen! Amen!'

'I is the shepherd of the sheep and the servant of the Lord,' Bee say. 'And if we must worship . . .'

'Beautiful Lord!'

' . . . If we must worship, we must worship in Spirit . . .'

'And in truth, Jeesus!'

'If we must worship we must worship with a ringing of the bell and bringing of our souls with a joyful noise unto the Lord . . .'

'Ooh Lord!'

'Who is greater than the Lord?'

'Yeeah!'

'. . . for he will carry out . . .'

'Yees!'

'. . . and he will bring you. He will search you and he will turn you . . .'

'Jeesus!'

'. . . He will touch you with his right hand.'

'Oh God!'

'Lift up your voices, oh ye hills!' Bee cry out.

'Yeees, Leader!'

'Lift up your voices, oh Jerusalem! Lift up your voices, oh Judah! Lift up your voices, Israel! Lift up your voices, oh Ethiopia! Lift up your voices . . .'

'Yeees!'

And now with the congregation answering him, Bee voice was getting stronger, and all the sadness and anger in his soul poured down in his words. The rain was falling and the church was leaking and the brethren was humming deep in soft rhythm to Bee preaching, and all of us was moving and the church was a sea and we was the boats rocking sweet, and I could hear It coming, I could hear It. I could hear all the angels coming in my ears with their wings shhhing like a storm of whispers. And heads was bobbing and hands was clapping and the church was rocking and the church was jumping, the church was shaking and humming, and Bee there on the pulpit, his voice ringing out to the four corners of the church above the rain and humming.

Like a strong wind, like a mighty water, like a river of fire, like a thousand doves with wings. It come, the Spirit. And I was clapping my hands and singing. And it catch Bee up and spin him round and bow him down and It hold him up and walk him down from the pulpit to the Centre Post. And he take up the bell and he ring it to the East and he ring it to the West, and to the North he ring it and to the South, Jeesus! And he take up the bowl of flowers with the holy water and sprinkle it over the congregation and he turn and walk down to Old Mother Raymond, Bolo mother, and hold up her hands and salute her in the Spirit, and her Spirit take her up and she begin to talk to him in unknown tongue. And in between the humming and the jumping, Sister Lucas, a round, plump black woman in blue, get up trembling, walk to them and she balance on one leg and she step off in that sweet, graceful, noble walk that black women alone have from generations of carrying on their head buckets of water and baskets of cocoa, and she go to the Centre Post and she spin and she twist and she turn and she ring the bell and fall on her knees and she pray to the Lord and her Spirit pick her up and she talk her language and she dance around like a bird going to fly, and I get up and go and meet her and my Spirit come on me, and all over the church people was getting up with their Spirit on them and we meet there in the centre of the church and we hold hands and salute one another, and we was there, the whole church, rocking and humming and talking our language, and the bell was ringing and water was sprinkling and the Spirit was in charge and I was shaking and shouting, Ooh God.

Then we was singing a hymn, soft and low, sweet with our rhythm:

> *The Lion of Judah shall break every chain*
> *And bring us to victory over Satan again.*

Then it cool down, die away with sweet, soft humming and low moaning, and a cleanness and a lightness come over the church, and the rain stop falling, and we was fresh and wash like new grass in the morning. I look 'round, and faces was smiling, and when I look at Reggie only his teeth was showing. I was sorry Bolo wasn't here to see it, to see Bee on the pulpit, to see the people how we rise, how we rise up, how we dance and sing and how we break the law like the law was nothing.

5 Bolo and Prince

When you break the law, you don't hurt the law, you don't change the law, you just make the law more the law; you stiffen the heart of the magistrate and set yourself to dodge and peep and every step you make, look over your shoulder for the police. But we *did* break the law.

And now that we taste again the sweetness of a real Baptist service, now that we feel again the thrill of ringing the bell, catching the power and shouting hallelujah from our souls, we can't go back to worshipping in the lifeless Catholic or Anglican way. So we go on, forgetting police and magistrate, preaching the Word, singing the hymns and catching the Spirit. We didn't go out and call anybody, but the word get around to people, and some of the old congregation come back now to be with us in the church again. It was nice, with the men holding up their heads in front their women and children, and Bolo there in the front row, singing with his voice, holding his body tall, still, giving us his self, his strength, a warrior on the battlefield again. It was nice in a dangerous kinda way for we know that any day Prince could attack. And he attack one day. Bolo wasn't there.

There in the middle of the hymn-singing and the shouting and the hand-clapping, with Sister Isabel bobbing beautiful in the Spirit, with Bee rocking sweet on the pulpit in a half-smiling surrender, and old Brother Theophilus shouting hallelujah, and Sister Lucas standing on one leg by the Centre Post, ringing the bell, ba-lang! ba-lang! ba-lang! to the four corners of the church, and I humming low as the Spirit drift me away, and all of us so full up with the sweetness of the service that we forget that we in the midst of Babylon, the police slip in the church and we didn't see them. Then, across the music of our joy, cutting through the God-praising, we hear this whistle blast and this gruff voice announcing: 'Awright, you under arrest!' And Bee eyes widening and the congregation coming back to itself, the handclapping and the God-praising ending and the bell in Sister Lucas hand still ringing though she ain't ringing it, and when we turn around, I see stand up there by the door this tall, bowleg, big-head man with a baton in his hand and a gun on his waist, and his eyes smiling in his wicked face.

'Don't try to get away. We have you now,' he say. And behind him, the other police stand up like a shield blocking the door, their batons raise up, ready for murder.

'Brethren, please don't run,' Bee say, his forehead frowning and his noseholes widening. 'Please don't give them the excuse to brutalise you.'

But, fear. Some of the congregation was rushing to the side doors for escape. That was a mistake. Police was waiting there for them too, and send them rushing back in the church screaming and trampling down one another. It was confusion, with people falling down and bawling and I in a corner gripping my two small children, my voice screaming, and Bee on the pulpit trying to calm the people, lifting up his voice above the confusion and shouting, 'It is good to give thanks unto the Lord and to sing praises to His name.'

And we too frighten to even answer 'Amen.'

And Corporal Prince saying, 'Shut your mouth, Dorcas. This meeting over. You under arrest.'

And Bee asking, 'For . . .? For worshipping my God in Spirit and in Truth?'

And Prince saying, 'Tell that to the magistrate. Round them

65

up, constables.'

They drag Bee down from the pulpit. They jab us with their batons. They form us in a line.

'The children? You arresting the children too?' Bee ask.

Prince put his hand on his hip, push up his chest and look us up and down. 'Take everybody,' he say. 'Let them come and see what inside a police station look like.'

We walk down the hill, with the police around us. We walk down the hill slow, right to the police van below.

'Inside!' Prince say.

'You going to cram all of us in there?' Sister Ruth scream. Sister Ruth is a big Trojan woman, and she plant herself in front the van.

'You want to walk to the station?' Prince ask. He look at Bee. 'You could walk, you know.'

Bee didn't say nothing.

'Then we will walk,' Prince say. 'Let us go.'

So now with one police driving the van behind us and the rest of them around us, we start to walk to the police station. Bee is in front with the elders, I behind with the women and children, and Corporal Prince marching off to the side of us like a conquering hero returning with his prisoners from battle. Lord, you really make us see trouble. But we go. Sister Isabel, her thin, wailing voice, screeching, burst out in a hymn. Sister Ruth join her and Bee take it up and all of us, prisoners, begin to sing:

> *I never get weary yet*
> *I never get weary yet*
> *Forty long years I work in the field*
> *And I never get weary yet.*

We walk through the village, with the hymn in our mouths and our rhythm and spirit, singing with our vexation and frustration as a cry, a shout to Jesus somewhere who forsake us too often, who turn us loose in this wilderness of brutes for police to beat and for the rulers of the land to swing us up, to swing us down like we is clown. Singing, calling on this same Jesus so that even if he deaf he will hear, we walk through the village with the people standing up to watch us pass, some giggling nervous, some shaking their heads and grinding their teeth, watching us with their eyes, with their sighs. We walk through the village with our song climbing over the trees, filling up the open space. Then, as we turn the corner by the market to go up to the police station street, we see a crowd waiting. To the side of it is Ivan Morton and a little way in front, in the middle of the road, with his shoulders draw up, his body plant sideways and his two feet apart, one a little in front of the other, is Bolo, holding his hands down at his sides like a stickfighter waiting on the drums to begin the battle.

'Stop!' Corporal Prince say, when we reach a few feet away from the crowd. And we stop, and our singing die away; and quick, a silence fall on all the people because Corporal Prince is walking up to Bolo.

Slow, stiff-leg like one dog inspecting another, Prince walk up to Bolo and look him over from head to toe, with that same careful tallness dogs show when they face a stranger. Nearer and nearer to Bolo he go as if he not only want to see him with his eyes but to smell out his maleness, check if there is fear in him – more than that, to give off his own smell of fearlessness and power and dangerousness so maybe he could cow him, bow him down so there wouldn't even be the need for battle. And Bolo stand up there in the middle of the road, tall, stiff, his mouth half open as the other fighting dog giving off a low, growling warning from deep inside his belly, announcing his own sharp dangerousness and readiness for battle.

Prince get that message and he turn and look across the road. We look too, and there coming forward is Ivan Morton.

'What happen, Corporal?'

'I am arresting these people.'

'For what?'

'It is against the law to worship as Baptist, Mr Morton.'

'Well, I suppose you have to carry out your duty.'

'Yes, sir.'

And with that Ivan Morton gone.

Prince turn to Bolo, but is Bolo who talk first.

'Where you carrying these people?'

Prince move back a step as if to see Bolo better, and now with his mouth push up and his face frown up and his head bend down like a bull a little, 'None of your business,' he say. 'Now . . .' but before he could finish what he begin, Bolo voice come out again: 'How you mean none of my business? I is a Baptist. These is my people. Look, you have my mother out there too. I want to know where you carrying my mother.'

'You have to get out the street,' Prince say, stiffening his body and bringing his feet together. And Prince have a gun on his hip and nine police behind him. 'Get off the street,' and Prince back away a step, his hand going down where the gun clip on near his waist.

And Bolo stand up there, bending like a cat a little. 'You going to shoot me down?' he ask Prince. 'You going to shoot me down for asking you a question? You going to shoot me down because I ask you where you carrying my mother?'

'These people going to the police station with me,' Prince say. 'Now get outa my way.' And Prince serious too and he bend forward his head a little, like a bull.

'She going to the police station with you? What she do?'

'What make you think I have to report to you?' Prince say. 'Get out the road. You want me to arrest you for obstructing an officer from his duty?' Prince ask, and his voice soft and full up with that dangerous politeness a man with power does show.

And Bolo voice low too, but low, holding back, controlling

his own rage and letting his dangerousness show. 'I don't want you to arrest me for nothing. What I want from you is what my mother do. She is seventy years. What she do? She thief? Who she poison?' And sudden so his voice burst out of him, 'What my mother do?'

'Listen,' Prince say, and Prince still cool, still calm, still comfortable in his own power, 'you obstructing the law. If you don't move . . .'

'If I don't move?' Bolo ask. 'If I don't move?' Bolo ask again.

'You *want* me to arrest you?' Prince ask, his voice firm and clear, carrying so all of us could hear. Maybe that was the time for Bolo to turn away, if he didn't want trouble, for Prince had a gun and nine police with him. But Bolo stand up there in the middle of the road, alone, tall now, and he look at Corporal Prince and in his voice now is this thing, this hard, trembling thing that tell you that he reach where he going and he ain't turning around and to get past him you will have to move over him, knock him down if you could.

'You want to arrest me?' Bolo ask, his voice so polite and soft.

But Corporal Prince ain't on the Police Force for seventeen years for nutten. He come face to face with many men before, and he seen men stiffen like the back of a cat in a corner with no place to run and who ain't thinking of running either and the only way to prevent a battle is if you turn away; and Prince know that he ain't turning away from Bolo, not in front all these people. Prince is a big man too, six foot three, thick hands, and back broad like a tapana tree, even if you forget the gun on his hip and the nine police in the back of him.

'You want me to arrest you?' Prince ask again, in his softest words, wondering a little, holding his hands away from his body as if he want to show that he ain't have to depend on the gun.

Bolo that time have his back bend forward a little and his

69

feet spread out with his weight on them, like a cat, his elbows turn out and his hands close to his hips as if is he with the gun and not Prince, and his knees trembling and his lips shaking and I could see it coming. I could see it. I could see Bolo ready and Prince readying himself and the policemen straightening and the men in the crowd holding their breath so as not to show their hard breathing, and Taffy by my side trembling as if he getting ready to fight too.

Then Prince was bending down his head like a bull, the veins on his neck straining, and his voice was so big in his throat that it come out like a scream so high and so low you couldn't understand what he was saying, but you didn't need to know for his big hands was moving out to catch hold of Bolo. And it was as if it was a dance the two of them perform before so that Bolo know already in advance what Prince was going to do, so when Prince hands grab for Bolo, Bolo wasn't there, but his head, his head was smashing into Prince face. He butt Prince and when Prince didn't fall down, he butt him again. Before Prince could hit the ground, the nine policemen was on Bolo with their batons swinging, and Bolo was there alone battling, butting and kicking and cuffing alone until a baton catch him on the jaw and one split his head and the policemen beat him down in a rain of blows. The women was screaming and I with them and my body was trembling and I was cold all over and I see Taffy – his eyes widening as he watch his father and the other men and realize that they not going to rescue Bolo – make a move to go to join the fighting. Same time Prince stand up with his revolver pointing at the crowd and the policemen have Bolo on the ground, kicking him, beating him, and Taffy rushing in, so I throw myself on him and Sister Ruth and Oliver and Miss Carol help me hold him down.

Then Bolo stop kicking out and cuffing. The police bend down and four of them lift him, one at each shoulder and two at the legs, and nobody holding up his head, and dash him on the floor of the prison van. They cram us into the van with him and they drive off to the police station, with Bolo stretch out on the floor, blood covering his face, his head lean to one side, one hand on his chest and the other over his head. Everybody was quiet, and the men turn their eyes away from Bolo, and didn't look at each other neither.

And going home from the police station after they let us go on our own bond, and Bee looking straight in front of him, and I at his side holding the hands of the two small children, still trembling from all that happen this evening. And the sun gone down, and the land darkening.

'I wish I was a man,' Taffy say, bending down and taking up a stone and flinging it into the half darkness, breaking the silence we was walking home in.

'Stones don't have eyes, boy,' I tell him. 'Suppose you hit somebody?'

'If you was a man what would happen?' Bee ask, his voice low, not looking at Taffy.

'Just be glad you not a man in these times, boy,' I say.

'All o' you . . .' Taffy say, his voice breaking out of him, 'all o' you stand up there and watch them beat him. And he was fighting for all you.'

'Boy, is you father you talking to?' I ask him.

'Leave him,' Bee say. 'Leave him.'

Walking home, and everybody silent again, and Taffy with his head down kicking at stones on the ground, kicking at stones as if he buy the shoes he was kicking them with. Taffy walking with his hands in his pocket, restless, his head moving from side to side. Taffy, sixteen years old, short like his father, feeling his manness and helplessness. Walking home, candle-flies bobbing in the air, the moon coming up, slicing the clean, white clouds under the sky, and Taffy with his head down, kicking at stones on the ground and grumbling to himself.

'Taffy!'

'Yes.'

'Who you answering "yes"? You so full up with manishness that you don't know how to talk to people.'

'Yes, Ma.'

'Boy!' And I look at my son growing to a manhood that is his own only if he have the power to take it, and there is so much that he don't understand. 'Boy, the law is not only the police you see in uniform here today. The law is the judges and the magistrates and the British soldiers. The law is the whole empire of Britain.'

Walking home, and Taffy ain't saying nothing, his head down, then sudden so as if a shock hit him, he lift up his head, his voice full with such surprise he start stammering, 'So ... so we can't ever fight? They going to keep on ... keep on doing us whatever they like, and we going to keep on taking it so? We not going to ever fight?'

And I wish Bee would tell him something about the battles that we fight already, about things that a boy Taffy age can't know. I wish Bee would just say something so the boy would know what to do. But Bee there walking with his head straight and his eyes in front of him as if he want the boy to keep up his vexation, as if deep inside his heart he want the boy to turn rebellious even if it mean going against him too. I look at Bee, but Bee have his eyes straight and his jaw bulge out, and he planting his feet down with that stiff, steady, hurting walk of a man bearing a funeral coffin, his body stiffening as if he prepare to take the blame, to be a nothing in his own child eyes. And I ... I ain't saying nothing, leaving Taffy question to hang in the air.

After that day we had other church services, but the Baptist church was never the same again. The shouting and the bell-ringing come to an end, and only a few people come together to praise God and sing the hymns in the tired Anglican and Catholic. It wasn't nice at all, and I know just now Taffy would go away.

They would try Bolo and sentence him to three years with hard labour in jail, but even before that, we would have a charge to answer in front the magistrate. What we going to do? Run away? Run where?

The nineteen of us walk up to the courthouse on the hill next to the police station and the jail. We go in and we sit down. We have no lawyer to plead our case, so one by one we go and stand up in front this red-nigger magistrate sitting down high up, like God, with his face puff up like a frog that vex for seven days and his lips clamp down like the two saucers of a oyster.

They read the charge and the magistrate look down his spectacles at us and screw up his face.

'Not guilty,' we say. And Bee talk. Bee say that he can't understand how in this country with so many different people, where they have religions for Hindu and Moslem and Anglican and Catholic, how it could be a crime for black people to worship as Spiritual Baptist. Bee ask: Is it because our religion ain't come from England? Bee ask: Is it because we ain't have no cathedrals and white priests? Bee talk. And when the magistrate couldn't take no more, he shout, 'Stand down!' And I swear his puff-up red-nigger face was going to burst.

'I am ashamed of you,' the magistrate say. 'You have the gall to stand up and argue when all you doing is leading these poor people astray, making them jump and prance and shout to the devil as if you still in the wilds of Africa.'

'Stand down!' he shout again, when Bee get up to argue, 'before I charge you with contempt of his Majesty's court.'

'I will reprimand and discharge you people,' the magistrate say when he cool himself down a little. 'I understand how this demigod could lead you astray, but you must understand that no civilized country will allow you to worship in this barbarous, heathen way. As for you, the ringleader,' he say, and he take a sip of water from the glass in front of him on the table, 'I

73

charge you ten pounds or twenty-one days. One week to pay.'

Ten pounds! Ten pounds and one week to pay!

So we had to sell the cow.

The two Indian men come in a broken-down yellow van with the bonnet tie down with a piece of copper wire. They stop at the standpipe at the corner, untie the wire, lift up the bonnet and pour a bucket of water in the radiator, then they back the van into the yard. Bee was there waiting for them, and they went with him down to the cowpen. They look at the cow. They squeeze the breast, peep under the tail, watch the teeth, then look at Bee and nod their head and pay him the money. One of them sneeze. They back the cow up a flat piece of board into the van, then the two of them get in the front and drive away, leaving Bee standing up in the yard, holding the money in his hands and watching the cow go away.

'We still have the calf,' I tell Bee to try and cheer him up that evening. But it had no cheer to cheer up Bee that day or any day for weeks and months to come; for it was not the cow alone. It was Bolo on the floor of the police van with his head lean to one side and the blood on his face, and he (Bee) don't know how to look at him. It was Winston gone away to be a police, is Taffy restless and vex and the smaller ones' eyes with questions that we can't answer. It was the church gone back again to a kind of worship we didn't like and didn't suit our spirit. It was the police and this country and this war that wouldn't end and people going away from each other, becoming strangers to each other right here with each man fighting for himself. It was everything. And what to do? What to do?

Now on an evening when Bee come home from the garden, was like a fire blazing inside of him. He can't sit down a minute, he must find something to do to keep him going. He cut the grass in the yard, he repair the cowpen, fix the latrine that was leaning, clean the drains, rip off the kitchen door and nail it up again, break down two steps and put in two new ones;

and I ain't telling him nothing, just watching him, just hoping that he get enough things to cut up and break down and fix back again to keep him going until he burn out whatever it is blazing inside him.

That was a bad year all around. The children, like they don't have eyes to see what happening, ain't doing nothing to make life easier for me.

And Reggie. You would expect because Reggie have a chance to win a college exhibition he would study his lessons so he could be somebody. No. Reggie want to be a cricketer. Reggie want to be a highjumper and he want to throw knife like Taffy all together. And of late now he take up to going down the bay to Buntin shop where the men of the village gather on a evening to play draughts and drink and talk about the war and Hitler and Churchill.

Buntin shop going to pieces. He giving credit and people not paying him, and Buntin don't even look like he care how his business go once the men come in his shop to talk stupidness about the war or God or Marcus Garvey.

What happen to Buntin? Or is so black people stupid? Chin, the Chinee shopkeeper have a shop with tins and bottles on the shelf, with cheese and butter and sugar and flour and black-eye peas behind the counter, and now with money flowing in Bonasse from people working on the Base, Chin making a addition to his place so in a few weeks he would be selling shirts and pants and dress and shoes. Buntin have pictures on his shelf: pictures of Marcus Garvey, Joe Louis, Jack Johnson and Haile Selassie. Buntin have on his wall, below his empty shelves with brown paper bills on wire hooks making cobwebs over his head, a sign he write himself:

> I am black and comely
> O ye daughters of Jerusalem,
> As the tents of Kedar
> As the Curtains of Solomon

Instead Buntin try to collect the money people owe him, he sit down in front his empty shelves with his foot cross and his forehead frowning, nodding his head away, listening to the discussions that go on in his shop every day. As Sister Ruby say, that is why we can't get ahead as a race of people. Talk, we like too much talk.

And Reggie. No matter how I talk to the boy, he insist on going to spend my money at Buntin who don't have all the goods in the first place and if he have it, you have to pay a cent or penny more than it cost at Chin. But Reggie want to listen to freedom talk too. He want to be there among the men to hear big-man talk and come home with a lot of stupid questions to puzzle my head. Who is Toussaint L'Ouverture? Who is Marcus Garvey? Who is Booker T?

What a little boy like that want to know these things for? In school they have things in books to learn, and if they want you to know who Garvey is or Toussaint or the other one, Booker whatever is his name, they will put it in the books. But the little boy listening to Buntin, who sit down there telling every boychild who come in that he, the child, is a prince, showing where it say in the Bible, . . . Ethiopia shall stretch forth her wings unto God and Princes shall rise forth out of Egypt . . . have Reggie coming home walking straight and tall without the goods I send him for, telling me he is a prince. But as I tell Reggie, and I will tell this to anybody, this ain't Egypt. And you could come from all the kings and queens of Egypt and Ethiopia put together, you still have to eat, you still have to get a job, and if you don't want to dig dirt for a living or pick coconut on Richardson Estate, you have to learn what they teach you in school. For Buntin could talk till his black face get blue, he ain't the governor or Captain Cutteridge who they send from England to write the books the children learning from in school. I didn't like how things was going at all. And just as I prophesy and say, Taffy stab a boy in the week before

Easter and run away to stay with his uncle in Port of Spain. Was like a blight fall on us that year.

I want to tell Bee: let's leave this place. Let's go down to the oil fields or to Arima, somewhere, anywhere where you could get a job or a piece of land and forget this place. Let's go somewhere where the smaller children could get a good school to go to, and Joyce could meet a nice young man to get married. Is only three children left and you and me, and we could make out. We could make out. The land you working now ain't bringing in that much anyway, and the house we living in ain't no mansion, and with the cow gone to pay the court, where we going to get money to repair it? Let's leave it and go, at least for the children sake. Joyce don't complain but she is a young lady, and I know she must be tired staying in this house every day, looking through the window at the few people passing. Let's go. If things don't work out for you right away I could get a job in somebody kitchen or washing clothes or something, something, and we could rent a house and start again without the police and the church and all this confusion living.

But I ain't tell Bee nothing, for where to find this place?

Then, as if God see that we couldn't take more pressure, not long after Easter, Germany surrender, then America drop the atomic bomb on Japan and the war was over. The war was over and we had Carnival again. The war was over and the Yankees, thank God, was leaving Bonasse, and at last we had a chance to get the church back to itself again.

6 Elections

Now with the war over and the Americans going back where they come from, it look like we had a chance for the village to come back to itself again; but I guess things don't come back ever to themself again. I guess when things so, they gone forever, like a day or a flower that fade away. Things go. And people forget too. I didn't know it that time but by the time the war end, we in Bonasse was a different people. I guess you could say we was changing over the years, with people dropping out the church and our children going to their schools and learning their lessons. I guess you could say we was changing, with the Yankees in the island and the hustlers in the village and the gayappe and lend-hand dying and the people living a life every man for himself, the town life where you have to be smart, to lie and dodge and peep and cut your brother throat and watch your brother cut your own. In the end it was as if the whole thing was a trick that we play on ourself. It was as if we was trying to take something from our right hand without our left hand knowing; we would find that people didn't want to bring things back to what they use to be, they want to continue to be Catholic and Anglican to get a better job, to get a better school for their children; and we was still saying that we wanted to be free.

That year every day Bee and Charleau was down at Buntin shop talking about voting and they was thinking to ask Ivan Morton to write a petition to call on Britain to give us the vote. And Charleau was going so far as to say that we should break away from England and take over the country for ourself. You could imagine Buntin in his glee, ain't care to sell a thing, sit down behind his counter listening and watching the excitement building. But the excitement didn't have too far to build because without any fight or petition or anything, before that year end we get the news that everybody who reach twenty-one could vote in the next election.

Was the same day that Reggie who, preparing to sit the college exhibition examination, come with his voice inside his belly and tell me that he make tenth place in the Christmas term test.

Tenth? So I guess all the talk I talk to him go in one ear and come out the next.

'What you want to do, boy? Pick coconut for a living?'

'No, Ma,' he answer me.

'Where else you think you heading, coming tenth? What job you expect? With things as they going, just now you will need a certificate to get a job digging dirt.'

And his dimples rush to hide in his cheeks as he try to bury the smile springing on his face, as if he think is joke I making. I watch this boy, my son, with his eyes turn to the ground, and he really don't know what I talking about. He don't know that the world not going to be kind to him because he beautiful.

I hear the conch shell blow down the beach to say a boat come in with fish. I look at the boy. And I feel sorry for all of us. We push these children to this education. We stuff them with it. And we don't know what this education doing to the heart inside of them. But what else to do?

'Reggie!' And now he lift his head and look at me. 'You have to learn, boy. You have to learn.' I say; and as I go to turn away, I hear the calf moo, and when I turn to the sound, I see Bee coming fast up the road, with his hands swinging across his body like he want to get up more speed. From the distance I could see, because I know Bee – Oh, God, something gone

wrong again!

'Bee!' And I was running to meet him. And I was right upon him before I realise it was gladness in him and water rush to my eye to see how I can't even see.

'We get it, Eva. We get it,' he said, and throw his hands around me. 'We can vote now.'

And when he see the water in my eye, he think was because of the British and their damn election.

And already Bee is moving.

'Where? Where you going?' I ask him.

'I going to see Ivan Morton.'

'Why you don't change your clothes and eat a little something before you go?'

But no, he can't eat, he can't stay still. He have to go right away, so I watch him go, walking with his feet not hitting the ground, with that gladness springing in his heels, singing in his walk.

That night Bee come home from seeing Ivan Morton. I was in bed but I wasn't sleeping, and all in him is gladness overflowing. And in my heart I saying, Thank God! Thank God! This time we going to release from bondage.

'Bee!' And I know he wasn't sleeping either. 'Bee!'

'Eva,' he answer me, with all the years of sufferation and tribulation in his voice and not being able to face the children, not able to face Bolo, not able to face me, not able to face himself. 'Eva!' And I wish Bolo wasn't in prison, was here to hear the news, to see that the day reach when we have the power to put a man in the Council. I wish Bolo was here to see that waiting have it reward too so he could forgive the people, forgive Bee. 'Eva . . .' And I waiting for his words, and he turn and reach out a hand to hold me, and I roll over and lay my head on his shoulder and I didn't feel so old any more.

Those days was nice days. For the first time in I can't remember how much years, Bee was smiling and making jokes with the children and giving us a glimpse of how a man does be when he free; and for Reggie sake especially, I was really happy.

Those days was really nice, and we had a good Christmas that year. True, the big boys, Winston and Taffy wasn't home, but we had a little money and I buy a few toys for the children, for Gem and Reggie, and for Joyce I buy a dress and a pair of shoes so she could go pretty to the party Miss Roxborough was having in the Roman Catholic school on Boxing Day, and I get extravagant and buy a nice piece of white cotton to make a gown for Bee to wear the day he preach the sermon when the church get free.

Christmas day was nice too. Five o'clock in the morning I wake up to the cock-crowing and bird-whistling and the paran band singing outside the door. I wake up Bee and the children and put the rum out on the table and the slice pork and the pepper-sauce to go with it, and we wait until they start the second seranale as is the custom before Bee go and open the door and welcome in Miss Celia and Felix and Laddy and Sonny Carrera and Sam Harris and Cynthia. Oh, and they come in singing, singing so sweet this Christmas morning, and when they finish Bee say, 'Take a drink! Take a drink!' And Mr Felix say, 'We taking only one. We going since yesterday morning and we have to cover the whole village today.' So they sing another seranale and then they say, 'Okay, we'll take another drink.' So they take another drink and sing another seranale, and then they get up with the quattro playing and the shac shac shaking and everybody singing and go out the door, and all of us come out on the steps and watch them go down the street to the next house because they couldn't leave anybody out.

It was really a nice Christmas. And I cook a good lunch, chicken and crab and callaloo, and rum was on the table and a little wine, and the place was smelling nice with new paint and varnish and my new curtains and fresh flowers that Joyce put in a vase on the cabinet. After lunch we sit down together and talk and joke and laugh and all of us had a little drink. Later in the evening some young fellows from the village come over with a guitar and a shac shac and a mouth organ and a bottle and spoon to give us a few tunes. Nice boys. Miss Rita son and Hagin and the youngest one of the Jeffrey brothers and Aji and Jacko and Miss Harris son, Clyde. They didn't know much Spanish songs like the real paran band, but the boys had a lot of spirit, and they sing the little Spanish they know and fill in the rest with calypso and sentimental songs that play over the radio. They remain with us a good time too, drinking a little and singing. It was only afterwards that I find out why they singing so long. Something was going on between my daughter, Joyce, and the boy playing the guitar, Clyde, Miss Harris son. And after they gone, Joyce went out on the steps and watch the road and watch the road and when I ask her what she watching the road so for she get confuse. Reggie say, 'Clyde,' and is then I know. But it was nice.

In the night we had a good service in the church too. People turn out, not in multitude, but enough so when we sing the hymns we could hear voices going up to heaven. And though we sing in the way the law sanction, and didn't ring the bell, somehow, by some miracle, the Spirit was there in our voice, and though we didn't bring it right out, I could feel it near ready to come out as soon as we call it in the true way. That wasn't far away for soon we would have elections.

Early in the new year the government announce that the elections would be in September, and from the day we get that news, Bee begin working for Ivan Morton right down until election morning, going all over Bonasse and through Charlotte and Montevideo, sometimes with Mr Simmons, sometimes with Mr Riley, sometimes with Charleau, going from daybreak, covering every hill and trace, getting hoarse from talking and red-eye from so much night without a proper rest, but going, going, going like a engine, going with that fire in his voice and that belief, pleading and arguing and bullying to get people to vote for Ivan Morton.

Oh, the election was a fine battle. Fighting against Ivan Morton was Rufus George and Captain Richardson. Captain Richardson is the owner of the coconut Estate in Bonasse, and though he give out money left and right and have a few fools canvassing for him, he couldn't win – we had enough white-man rule already. But Rufus George was a different story. Rufus was tall, black, a ex-woodcutter with a voice like thunder and shoulders broad from his years of axing trees. Though he was from Charlotte, people in Bonasse knew Rufus well, for he was one of us, drinking with the men, pulling in seine with them. Rufus had in him a passion, a kinda vexation that when he stand up before a crowd he would get all tangle up with his words and his feelings. But Rufus don't have the edu-cation.

They tell this story, how one night at a meeting, Rufus was talking about the cost of living.

'People can't eat book in this country,' Rufus say. 'People can't eat words. What the people need is bread – B R E D – bread.'

'Rufus, you leave out the A,' somebody from the crowd call out to him.

And Rufus correct himself, 'B R E D – A.'

They tell of another time when the *Gazette* reporter come up from Port of Spain to interview Rufus for the newspaper about the harbour that Captain Richardson say they should build in Bonasse. The reporter tell Rufus that Mr Richardson suggest that they should put more buoys out in the sea to mark the area.

'Boys?' Rufus say. 'You could see that Mr Richardson don't know one thing about the Bonasse sea. Big, big men does drown out there in the sea and he want to put boys.'

No, we couldn't vote for Rufus. Charleau and Mr Buntin say that he didn't have no programme, if he get elected to the Council he wouldn't know what to do, Bee was saying the same thing too.

'Who we want in the Council is a man that qualify. What we want is a man with education just as the people in Britain. And we have that man here,' Bee say from the platform. 'A man who train as a teacher, who teach your children in the school, a man who could talk and take up your cause in the Council of the land.'

And Bee talk too about freedom and about the rights of a people to worship in their own religion. Bee talk, his voice bursting with all the tribulation and vexation that we suffer through the years, sometimes his voice going like thunder like he on the pulpit at church in front of the congregation. 'This is the man!' he would cry out. 'This is the man! Born right here, a man of knowledge and understanding to represent the people: Ivan Morton!'

Oh Jesus, and we would clap our hands and drown out thunder. And Ivan Morton would stand up from where he is on the platform and hold up the fingers of his right hand in a V for victory sign, like Winston Churchill, and he would walk out to the middle of the platform under the gas-light, holding his head straight and putting down his foot firm. And he would hold up his other hand with another victory sign and we would clap and clap until he put down his hand.

And talk! Ivan Morton could really talk. He say what holding us back is that we not getting proper education. He saw what we want is a chance and we would be as good as the whiteman. He saw we need more schools and we want old age pension and hospitals for the sick and a good health office and more exhibition places for the bright children and more jobs for the youth. He read from a paper in his hand. He quote facts and he give us figures. He talk and say we want a new governor, and when he finish talking he hold up his hands in two victory signs. Rufus was all right, but after you listen to Ivan Morton, you had to put Rufus aside.

Then was the night of the vote counting. Since evening, from all over the village, people surround Buntin radio to listen to the results coming in. And when we get the victory news, we give out a shout that wake up the whole village. Man, woman and child form a band and jump up in the road and dance and sing. Old Miss Sylvestre was crying like when she daughter get married, and Mr Simmons shoot off his gun in the air like it was New Year, and all over the place in the crowd, people was holding on to one another and kissing one another and shaking hands, and the little children who come out with their parents, feeling this thing from the people without knowing what was happening, was running up and down shouting and happy too.

'I tired,' Bee say when he come home from the celebration that went right through the night to next morning.

'You could sleep whole day today,' I say. And I was really glad to see this thing end so he could go in his bed and get a proper rest.

That Sunday, a lot of people turn out to church thinking that the law to make us free pass already, looking to shout and sing and catch the Spirit and ring the bell. But not yet. Bee preach a nice sermon that day. And though maybe we coulda get away with shouting and catching the Spirit, Bee say, 'Let us restrain ourselves today. Let today be the last worship in this heathen way. For today we have in the Council a man to plead our cause, to change the law, to right the wrong that going on against us for these long years. Let us workshop quiet tonight as we been worshipping these bitter years. Let our prayers be a mark of respect for the man we put in the Council. Let our hymns be a thanksgiving to God who lift us out of the pit, save us from the fiery furnace. For tonight the road nearly end, the battle nearly won, the river nearly cross. As St Paul say to the Corinthians, Let us run with great patience the race that is set before us.'

And we say Amen. We say Amen. Amen. Things was going to change. Our time was come.

And as if to clear the way for the change that was going to come in Bonasse, a month after the elections Captain Richardson, who own the big coconut Estate, put his land and house up for sale and went away to England. A American living in Port of Spain come up and buy the Estate, but nobody wanted the house, and for months it would remain on Bonasse hill between the three giant palmiste trees, with cobwebs growing on it, like a big white concrete tomb, a house people would begin to say is haunted. I for one didn't go near it in the night and, God knows, I really didn't care – if it stay right there and rot away.

7 Bolo Returns

When Bolo enter Buntin shop, Mr Buntin is sitting alone behind the counter the way he was those days – his chin in one hand and a pencil in the other, his bald head bend over some slips of brown paper, trying, I suppose, as a sort of consolation, to total up the amounts his old customers still owe him, so that when people come in and see the empty shelves he would be able to say: 'Look at these accounts! People owe me hundreds of dollars and they wouldn't pay. How you expect a shop to run so?' At that hour he wasn't expecting nobody, for those days, apart from sweets for the schoolchildren and the one or two or us who drop in now and again, the only customers to his place was the few old men who go there to talk politics and religion with him; but that was on evenings.

As he, Buntin, tell it later – for later when things start to happen that involve Bolo, people would talk. Everybody would have a story that he witness, to add to or to take away from what others say; so that though is true that every single body wasn't there to see every single thing that happen to Bolo, we, all of us, know his history just as if we was all there to see. Buntin lift up his head in the middle of one morning and see Bolo enter the shop with a quiet carefulness in his step. He sit down on a bench, not saying nothing, his eyes roaming over the shop, touching everything: the empty shelves, the unpaid accounts, stacks of brown paper slips that Buntin had hanging from wire hooks growing dust and cobwebs, the faded pictures of Jack Johnson, Joe Louis, Marcus Garvey and Haile Selassie, and the sign so faded that you could barely read:

> *I am black and comely*
> *O ye daughters of Jerusalem*
> *As the tents of Kedar*
> *As the curtains of Solomon*

so that Buntin, who didn't even have a bottle of rum for sale, feel sorry, feel guilty, feel that he owe it to Bolo to give him a explanation of what it is that happen in Bonasse in the years that he, Bolo, was in jail.

'Boy, things change. And then again, things ain't change,' Buntin tell him. 'Things gone to the dogs. People credit from me and leave without paying and gone to buy at Mitchell place. But I still here. Thank God.'

'Mitchell?'

'You don't know Mitchell open a snackette with a juke box in a corner and a girl to serve drinks? People leave me and gone there.'

And Buntin tell him about Ivan Morton winning the elections and moving to the big house that Richardson dead and left, about the hell people seeing without jobs and land to work and with the Estate paying next to nothing, and how if you want to get anything done you have to be a member of the party group that Ivan Morton form and that Mitchell running.

Bolo sit down and listen, Buntin say, with the same quiet carefulness that he walk in with, and for a long time he don't say nothing. And when he do talk, he talk slow, he talk as if each word is a stone, and he don't want the weight of the words to break his voice, had to let them out of his mouth careful, one by one; and he talk about the old times and the co-operation that use to be in the village. He say that now, he didn't care about Mitchell or Ivan Morton, all he want was to live and be a man, and he want a piece of land to work and a woman to settle down with. They talk about land and Buntin tell him that the government was giving out land to those who want to do farming. And Buntin tell him about Eulalie who gone to America to live, and both of them was sorry, and then it was lunch time and the schoolchildren drop in and buy sweets and Buntin send one of them to buy a flask of rum for he and Bolo to drink as a celebration, as a welcome. And Buntin feel good about buying the rum and he was glad that Bolo come just at that time, for talking with him make him feel sad, but it lift up his spirit, and that evening when the fellars come to talk about politics, Buntin pick up a broom and start to cobweb the shop.

After that first day, Bolo go by Buntin regular and Buntin sit down with him and together they make out a application for Bolo to lease a piece of the land that the government say they was going to give out to people who want to do farming. They put a stamp on it and send it to the office in San Fernando.

Two months pass and Bolo ain't hear a word about his application, didn't even get one of those little piece of paper that the government send in a brown envelope to tell you that they receive your application and was giving it consideration. Bolo didn't even get that.

'You should join the party group. Things will be easy for you,' Buntin tell him.

'I will go to the office and check up on the application,' Bolo say.

Bolo let another month pass before he go to the office in San Fernando. Brother Ambrose nephew work there. So between what Ambrose nephew say and what Bolo tell Buntin, it ain't hard to put together what happen there that day. Bolo reach the office early and what he meet there is a place where nobody care, where poor people line up since morning and the clerks not even watching across at them, busy doing nothing as if they not working, but there to wash their face and comb their hair and read newspaper, and if they know you or like your looks, they will come and ask you what you want, like they doing you a favour.

Bolo wait and wait in a line that was getting longer, and in front of him is this grey old man, short like a tree stump, in a oversize jacket, with his legs spread apart a little, as if they plant him there, as if somebody tell him, 'Stand up there and wait your turn,' and so he waiting there, this little man with the face of a mouse and a little foolish begging smile and his quick darting mouse eyes questioning and wondering, stopping anybody passing to ask, to make sure: 'This is the line where they tell you about your land? This is the agriculture office?' taking out from his pocket a paper again and again to show anybody who look like he could help him. 'This is the paper they send to me.' So one clerk go to the counter and attend to a few people, and at last this old man get to the head of the line and as he shove his hand in the pocket of his beat-up jacket, as his fingers bring out the paper, trembling, the clerk start to close the book; and the old man stand up there holding out the paper, and the clerk closing the book, and Bolo asking: 'What happen? What you doing?' and the clerk closing the book, not hearing, and the old man holding up the paper and looking at Bolo and the clerk beginning to move away.

None of us could blame Bolo. I know how it is with these officers. I see in Bonasse old people stand up whole day in the hot sun, waiting for the officer to come and give them the few dollars they get as old age pension, and when the office is ready to close for the day, somebody come out and say in this loud voice like the people they talking to deaf or stupid, 'Come back to-mor-row.' And the old people just get up and go. I know. But what you going to do? You make noise and police come and trouble.

'Listen, man, what you doing? You can't leave people here and go 'way just so.'

'You don't see is lunch time?' the clerk say. He is a brown-skin boy with a thin moustache and with his hair part in the middle, and he continue to walk away. Before he make two more steps, Bolo is by the counter and grab him by his collar, and he draw back his hand to hit him. Then he let him go. 'Okay,' Bolo say, 'Okay.' And he walk out the office.

'I glad you didn't hit him,' Buntin tell him. 'You'da get yourself in hot water.'

That was the end of Bolo and the land. They never write and tell him nothing about his application, and he never go back to find anything out from them.

Now in the village, Bolo see the girls with nothing to do and the young men going away every day to another part of the island, mostly to the city to find a job, going with the bongo dance in them and the wake songs, the blood, the guts, the little life the village still had in it, going, going; all that was staying was the old beat-down people.

On a evening he would come down to the shop, Buntin say, and sit down and listen to the fellars talk and he'd smoke one cigarette after another and hardly say a thing. Sometimes he would pick up himself and travel about the island: Port of Spain, Sangre Grande, Moruga; but every time he would come back with his eyes open, looking as if something was here in Bonasse for him that he couldn't let go, something here for him to conquer or to conquer him.

One day he tell Buntin, 'I feel as if time flying away and leaving me.'

'You's a young man,' Buntin tell him. 'What you would say if you was old like me.'

One day Buntin ask him, when he come back from one of his trips, 'What you want with this place? What you want in this small place?' And he didn't know. He didn't have any answer.

'You searching for something, what it is?'

It was as if he was searching for something, like a woman, Buntin say. But it wasn't a woman, it was his life he was looking for.

Then Carnival come.

Each year the Carnival we have in Bonasse was getting more and more like the one they have in Port of Spain, with steelbands playing music on the street and masqueraders dress up in pretty costumes that cost forty and fifty dollars. Now we had we own Carnival Development Committee, and we stage a Steelband Competition and a Calypso Competition, and we had a Queen show like in Port of Spain, with Mitchell as the Master of Ceremonies and with Ivan Morton there to give one of the girls a kiss and to crown her Bonasse Carnival Queen. With all this, the stickfights is one thing that ain't change.

When Carnival come is like a call go out to all the men. Is as if something from deep inside them wake up and want to face a danger, and they leave whatever they doing and go again each year to the place where they have the gayelle, the ring. Every year they go to shed their own blood or to bust somebody head. And for what? I ask Bee. For the bottle of rum and the five dollars that Mitchell offer to the man to bust the first head? For nothing, he tell me. No. Not for nothing. Because they is man.

'Because,' say Buntin, 'because they is men. They must test theyself against each other in this dangerous battle, so as to keep alive the warrior in them, in us, to show us again that we have champions, that we have men.'

And is to see this test that carry Buntin to the gayelle that now locate in front Mitchell snackette for him to see what the village have to offer that year.

All the old champions was there, Mr Buntin say: Riley and Pretty Foot and Joe Tamana, a old man from River Road who hands was so quick they say his stick had on it Shango, the Spirit of Lightning; and Sam Botey and Rajkumar, a old Indian who was a terror in his time both in the Creole stickfighting and in gadkhar that the Indians fight with two sticks; all of them come to be together as the elders of the tribe to take a drink and to remember their days and to see what the young ones will show.

A lot of young fellows was there who Buntin know: Sonny Marshall and Lazare, not great stickman but if the drums beat good and the rum get to their head they will go into the ring. And Innocent was there and Big Brother and Short Boy who in his day could fight with the best, but who head now over the last few years was a target for stickmen, because he drink too much and he too brave and he don't have again the speed of body and the sight to watch a blow coming down and at the last second slip outside it and in the same action send in his own terrible reply; so he was easy now, soft, a bobolee for men to beat. But Short Boy wouldn't retire and he would go back again and again every Carnival, and even after they bust his head, he would still want to fight. Stickmen who know him in his days would hold him and console him and beg him to stay out the ring; and he would shake his head, yes, with his tears but the drums would beat and with tears still wet on his face Short Boy would enter the ring again. And there too is Manny and Parker and Matthew Raymond, the one who is the champion, and a few others – Sam Merino and Godwin and Little Man.

Little Man was something like Short Boy except that he was more dangerous. Little Man was never a champion, but when he was drinking he couldn't hear a drum beat if he didn't jump in the ring. And you had to be very careful with him because he was tricky. The moment you take your eyes off him he would strike. That way he cut good, good stickman. Once he cut somebody, Little Man would drop his stick and run far from the gayelle until after another bout of drinking, then he would come back again.

And it have spectators plentiful watching as if they come to look for something to remind them of who they is.

So everybody is there at the gayelle in front of Mitchell

snackette. Everything is ripe for battle. The drummers beating, and the chantwells is singing this song that is to stickmen the terrible lamentation and anthem and invitation and warning:

> *Today today*
> *Today today gran funeral*
> *Today today gran funeral*
> *Today today gran burial.*

But no stickman enter the ring. Then Riley and Pretty Foot go in against each other not in serious, but as a right, a honour, because they is old heroes. Slow and awkward with their age, they dance around in the ring, and one of them make a blow that the other parry and then they hug each other and go out the ring. And now is the serious time.

Matthew Raymond go in. A tall giant of a man, Matthew Raymond is the present champion not through any beauty of movement or swiftness but on the strength of his hand. A slow, sure, cautious man, his dance just a shuffle and a limp and a coming in like a tank without no driver, Matthew Raymond would parry, parry, parry until he see a chance to strike and then he would bring his sledgehammer hand down with all his might. If you stop the blow, the power behind it could break your stick or send a splitting shock through your elbows; and he cut many stickmen just by forcing down with his blow their own sticks onto their head.

Matthew Raymond stay in the ring a long time, showing off his might in a clumsy dance, Mr Buntin say, leaning back, sliding his stick through his hands, shifting around and changing positions, leaping up to strike and sliding back to parry, all in a mock display to encourage somebody to come in against him. And the chantwells to bring out his boast over the gayelle, sing:

Ten thousand to bar me one
Me one me one.

It look like nobody wanted to go in and fight him. And the drummers beating like crazy and the chantwells singing songs to shame fellars who say they is stickmen. And the crowd is restless and everybody talking and the old stickmen look on, shaking their heads and grumbling, ashame to see the crop of stickmen who stand there taking a drink, laughing a little too loud, and some of them singing along with the chantwells without shame, the songs that should urge them into the ring.

So you could understand, Buntin say, how this boy, this young fellow, Miss Elaine son, the last one, the one they call Lester, a boy not more than seventeen years, would break 'way from his friends and jump into the gayelle, snatch up a stick and dance around to the drums. Before he had time to realize what he was doing and to change his mind and get out the ring if is a joke he was making, those stickmen who all the time was standing around without shame now suddenly get brave and anxious, and Sam Merino and Innocent and Big Brother was jostling with each other to be the one to fight him.

And now sudden so, Innocent was right up in front of this boy, holding his stick over his shoulder ready to give him battle. And outside the ring the old stickmen who could see, who know that this is just a young boy caught up by the drums is calling to him to come out, and his friends who still can't understand what madness seize Lester is shouting to him too. But it have others who glad for a free show, who want a battle no matter at who sorrow. They shout: 'Leave him! Leave him! Let him fight!' And the boy there in the confusion stand up holding his stick up over his head, backing away from Innocent and bending back from his waist like he trying to do a limbo dance, but he was moving too slow, and without the

95

rhythm, now that Innocent was in front of him and the drums was beating, as if at last he realize what trouble he is in.

And Innocent in front this boy is king. He dancing slow in a tall triumphant rhythm, Buntin say, shifting his body and peeping out his head with not too much caution because he know that this boy backing away from him is easy pickings. So he ain't in too much hurry, he could afford to take his time to dance and look pretty, bending down low and coming in from the right and coming in from the left, pushing his stick forward from his elbows and pulling it back to scare and confuse the boy who going back, going back to the edge of the ring. And Innocent turning him, turning him till we have him with his face to the sun. And the boy there don't have sense enough to drop the stick and run. He have too much bravery in him, so that even those who want him to run, don't want him to run, want him to make some miracle and defeat Innocent. And as if he feel this too, feel that his own braveness is worth whatever price he have to pay, he stop backing away and face Innocent with his stick high over his head and his eyes squinting because of the sunlight, and bracing himself to strike a blow or to block one, and Innocent lifting his stick now and the singing going on:

> *Boisman don't know*
> *Boisman don't know the danger*
> *Boisman don't know the danger*
> *Boisman don't know the enemy.*

And the boy with the sun in his eyes, pushing his stick up and bringing his head under it waiting, and the blow from Innocent coming down, coming down and the boy pushing his stick waiting for the clash of wood. But Innocent is too high up on his toes and when his blow fall, it catch the boy way in the back of his head. The boy stagger and his blood pitch and his friends rush and hold him up and lead him out the gayelle, asking him, 'Why, why, Lester, why you go in?' And now with blood in the ring and the crowd buzzing with the animal wanting and the drums beginning to blaze afresh and the singers to pour out their song, Innocent dancing his might, turn and find Bolo in the ring in front him. If Innocent didn't want to fight before, he know that he must battle Bolo now or be a coward in front of the whole people.

So now Innocent shake his stick above his head, bend down, go into his stance and begin his dance to show off his beauty, to make his own boast before he turn to face Bolo who in another corner of the ring is dancing his own dance, making his challenge. And now the two of them face each other.

If Innocent is frighten, he don't show it; he come in fast in a shuffling searching dance trying to turn Bolo to face the sun, but every time he make a move, Bolo move with him. And so they go, with Innocent trying to circle and Bolo moving with him in a tight and dangerous dance. And Bolo know 'bout the sun, Bolo know the length of a stick and the distance he must stay to be clear of a man, and Bolo ain't frighten, and Bolo coming in slow and fast and smooth with his shoulders drawn back and his stick protecting his head and the full length of his body, and his weight on his waist and his eyes looking at Innocent moving around in that careful shuffling dance, his stick in his right hand in front of his face and his left hand holding up one leg of his trousers and his eyes watching Bolo feet, how they moving. And Bolo sliding in, sliding in smooth with his left foot pushing out from under his stick and his right foot coming up behind it smooth and careful and sure. And Innocent going back and moving to the side in his careful shuffle, keeping outside the range of Bolo stick; and Bolo dancing in on him, not so much forcing him back, but giving him less and less of the ring to manoeuvre in, so you know that soon Bolo would have him in a corner. And now to drive Bolo back, Innocent straighten himself and begin to twirl his stick wild over his head as if he going to hit out any time, but Bolo keep coming in like a wave with that soft hard flowing rhythm, coming in with that slow sure sliding dangerousness, his eyes open watching everything, and the drums beating and the chantwells singing and the people holding their breaths inside them, watching Bolo coming in and Innocent trying to drive him back.

Then quick, as Bolo go to close in, his stick raise to strike, Innocent stop moving and, grinning as if the whole thing is a joke from the beginning, a mock thing like what happen between two old stickmen who just want a chance to show off and remember their beauty in front of the village (but with no intention to do real battle) he hold up his hands, throw down his stick and move to embrace Bolo in a kind of surrender.

'No! No!' Bolo say, tugging away, refusing the surrender. 'No. Battle! Battle!'

And Bolo move back to give Innocent space to take up his stick and ready himself again. But Innocent, as if he believe he could grin himself out of his shame, leave his stick on the ground and melt into the crowd, all the time grinning.

Bolo vex now because he come to fight. But he take up his stance again and himself begin a new chant to make the other stickmen shame:

> *Crow crow jumbie-bird crow*
> *Jumbie-bird wouldn't crow.*

And he gone back in the ring alone and start dancing boastful, strong and dangerous, doing everything to make them come and fight him. And the same stickmen who was hot to fight the boy Lester, and Matthew Raymond, the champion, all of them stand up there watching him dance the length and breadth of the ring with his tough beauty and grace while the drums beat and the chantwells sing:

> *Crow crow jumbie-bird crow*
> *And the jumbie-birds wouldn't crow.*

Not one of the stickmen would go in.

The crowd watching start singing the chorus too, sinking the words into the stickmen ears making them taste their own cowardness.

And sudden now as if a wisdom hit him, Bolo stop dancing; and the chantwells stop singing and the drummers beating stop and everybody look at Bolo.

'So nobody going to come in the ring?' Bolo say. And the stickfighters there, some taking a drink, some watching their stick, some holding their wrist. 'So nobody ain't fighting?' he ask again with a cry, a shout, rage trembling his voice, making his chest swell. Was as if the whole thing send him crazy, Mr Buntin say, he lift his stick and bring it down on the face of one of the drums and cut it in two and he hit the same drum again, and then like a madman he move around slashing the drums with a rain of blows, and there in front of the whole village of men, he cut to ribbons the skin of every drum.

'Who don't like it come and beat me. Come and beat me,' he shout. 'Come!' And maybe they shoulda go against him there, that day. But, Buntin say, they stand up there, the whole village of them, and watch him, Matthew Raymond and Big Brother and Innocent and Sam Merino and a lot of others, but not a man raise a hand against him.

Bolo spit on the ground and as he turn to walk away Mitchell come out of his snackette and say: 'How you could mash up the drums, man? I pay these men to beat drums, Bolo. You want me to call police for you?'

'Call police,' Bolo say, 'but when I come out of jail, don't let me find you.' And Bolo walk away holding himself tall, making his stride long, leaving the people buzzing in confusion and the stickmen with their shame. This was a new Bolo we was seeing; that wasn't the end; we would see him again.

8   Badjohn

From that day it look to everybody that Bolo had one mission: to force the village stickmen to battle him, to make them face up to that man-challenge that they inherit from Fitzy Banrye and Musso and Joe Tamana and Riley and Wattley and all that long line of stickmen who carry on their warriorhood in this heathen country far away from Africa, bringing it out, parading it for the whole village, for the whole people to see on Carnival day; and so he would push and provoke not only stickmen but would harass and insult any villager to get him to rise up and battle him.

Right after Easter he decide that he want a job. He was done with climbing coconut trees for a living, and since he didn't get the land from the government, he had put aside the idea of farming; and as to fishing, he tell Buntin that he wasn't going out in the sea to drown in no little boat when so much people was living easy on land doing nothing. He want a job with the government, something easy.

'Times hard,' Mr Buntin tell him. 'County Council and Public Works laying off people every week. Men with years of service have to line up in the Public Works yard every Monday morning to hope that their name call so they would get a few days work for the fortnight.'

'They will give me a job,' Bolo tell him.

One day Bolo march into the big office where the officers sit down behind their desks and ask to see the engineer in charge of the department. Cash is the messenger but act as a kind of guard. Cash try to stop him. He knock down Cash and went straight into the engineer office with the sign PRIVATE mark on it. Nobody know what happen with Bolo and the engineer in the office, but next day Bolo was working as a watchman for the Public Works Department and at the end of the fortnight he draw his pay.

You could call that the beginning. In a few months he was a full terror in the village. Everybody stay clear of him. He walk with a gruff strength and vexation, as if hoping for somebody to offend him so he could slap or kick or butt, depending on who he had to deal with. And, Lord, he was strong. They say he had the strength of a madman when he was fighting. He alone could beat five ordinary men, and when he was drinking he could beat twelve.

He start now to drink every evening at Mitchell snackette, not paying a cent for anything, not there at Mitchell place or for that matter any place else in the village. He would go into Chin shop, order bottles of rum or beer or whatever goods or drink he wanted, and take it out – no money. At the market was the same thing: on Saturday evenings you could see him walking slow through the sheds that was Bonasse market, going from stall to stall, inspecting the goods people selling and when he was ready, taking a fish here, a piece of beef there, some tomatoes, mangoes, ochroes, whatever he want. Bolo didn't buy nothing. In time we in the market vendors grow to expect him, and some of the vendors call out to him even before he get to their stall to make him a offering of their best, keeping a competition going between themselves to see who could best satisfy him. I wasn't in that. I try to make a joke of it, but I didn't like it.

Nobody could satisfy Bolo, and the more people try to please him, the more pressure he put on them. And he had no stopping. It look as if he despise Bonasse people, as if every time he see a man, he want to cuff him down or kick him; and those of us who know him before he went to prison, had to say he was going crazy – though for me his craziness had too much sense in it.

Mitchell with the snackette was his special target. And though he drink free liquor at Mitchell snackette every evening, he was always pinching the girl Mitchell had working there and harassing the men having a drink and if they talk back, which is what he wanted, he would get the excuse to cuff somebody down. After a time people didn't want to go into Mitchell snackette once they knew that Bolo was in there drinking.

Mitchell had nothing to tell him, otherwise he would get a licking. Mitchell force a smile on his face and watch his business going down and Bolo sit down in a chair in his snackette, alone, like a lion that loose that nobody can't go near, and the juke box playing, and the electricity bill to pay, and the drinks on the shelf getting cobwebs because Bolo there. People make a joke of it. They say: 'Mitchell sell his snackette to Bolo.' And everybody watching to see what would be the outcome of the situation. But Mitchell not getting vex at all. Even people who didn't like Mitchell begin to marvel that he had so much patience; what it really is, is that Mitchell planning to kill Bolo. They sure that nobody can't take so much pushing without running amok one day.

Others say that Bolo is the one waiting for Mitchell to lose patience. That had to be true for Bolo do every wickedness he could imagine. He would kick down the table for no reason, he would break glasses on the floor, and sometimes he would invite Komono and all the other rascals in Bonasse who do nothing but drink rum whole day, and they would sit down and have a time, drinking Mitchell rum without having to pay and they would laugh loud and make a lot of noise and drive decent people away, and if the juke box wouldn't play a tune they would kick it and shake it until now the juke box come to be a half-dead piece of furniture in the corner, grating and scraping when people put money in it to play.

But still all Mitchell doing is coming into the snackette and forcing a smile, forcing a smile, then Mitchell couldn't force a smile no more: the girl he had working there leave the job, the place stinking, cobwebs spreading, the juke box not playing, nobody buying, and the time was near when if things keep on going so, Mitchell would have to close down the place. So the day come when Mitchell tell him something.

'Bolo, we is friends, eh,' Mitchell say, and his voice is begging and his little eyes blinking fast and he talking slow. 'You come in here, and you drink and I don't say nothing, not so . . .?'

And Bolo sit down there, Komono say, for is Komono telling us the story, sipping his drink, not even looking at Mitchell, and that time the place empty except for the same Komono who tell us the story. Komono is a half-Carib fellar who always drunk anyway and have on his head more bumps than a alligator have on its body, from beatings and falls so that not even Bolo could scare him away from drinking.

And Mitchell saying: '. . . but if we ain't learn to get along with one another like other people, how things will go . . .? How? Bolo, I don't think you's a bad fellar. I treat you good. I treat you like a brother. You come in here and call for drinks, I ever refuse you any? I ever ask you to pay a cent? For all the drinks you take, I ever take a penny from you? And you pinch the girl I hire to work and now the girl leave and gone, I tell you anything? I say "Bolo, don't do this, Bolo, don't do that." I tell you anything?' And Mitchell voice full with tears and is like he choking and he talking slow and his voice low low, and it look like he can't take no more and he reach the stage where he will pull out the cutlass people say that for months he sharpening every day and chop Bolo or take up himself and go away and leave the place for Bolo.

'You feel I should pay you?' Bolo ask him. And Bolo voice don't have a trace of sympathy. If anything, is like he wishing for Mitchell to draw his cutlass.

'No, no, not payment, Bolo, not payment,' Mitchell say in his same pleading way as if his patience have no end. 'But . . . but, man, I running a business. I have things to sell, and if people can't come in here and take a drink in peace, what going to happen to my business. You want me to close down?'

'I stopping your business, Mitchell?' Bolo ask. And Bolo is the one getting vex. 'I stopping your business?'

'Ain't nothing for you to get vex for, Bolo. I just telling you what happening.'

'You just telling me that you don't want *me* in your place. That's what *you* just telling me,' Bolo say.

'No, I just telling you that . . . Well, business . . . I have a business. I . . . I mean, other people want to take a drink.'

'And I preventing them? What you telling me Mitchell? That I is a beast, preventing people from coming inside your place?' Rightaway Bolo get in a rage and slam the glass he was drinking from onto the floor. 'I is a beast?'

'But that ain't nothing to get vex for,' Mitchell tell him. 'Sit down, man, and take a drink. I is your friend. Sit down, you ain't no beast.'

'You insulting me,' Bolo tell him, 'that is why I could never have peace in this place. Because you's a big shot you feel you could insult anybody.'

And, as Komono tell it, Bolo was happy for the opportunity. Just so his voice get big and his neck veins start to strain and Komono, who see these signals before, say that although he is a hero, he begin to look for the door. For Bolo pick up the chair he was sitting on and he fling it at the shelf and crash down the bottles, and he didn't stop. He move over the snackette smashing tables and chairs and beating the juke box and groaning and grunting and smashing. He was crazy that night, Komono

105

say, and when the police come, they find him on a stool, taking drink cool as ever and they see Mitchell in a corner crying long water, watching the break-bottles and the rum flowing and his place in pieces.

As soon as Bolo get out of jail he was back at it again. He was a lion in truth, loose in the streets. Even at the gambling club where the toughest men bet their money, Bolo would get into a card game they call Whappie and have everybody uneasy. None of the men want to really bet him because they was frighten to touch his money, but he put his money on the table and he call his bet and if they didn't bet him, that to Bolo was a offence, so they bet him. He didn't much care which card play, they say, as long as he was betting, and when he lose, he play crazy: he would sit and watch the men bet each other, then when at last he see enough money on the table, he would rise up, take his two hands, pull the money to him, stuff the bills in his pocket and go his way. 'Call police for me now,' he would say.

Nobody ever try to stop him. Every time this happen, Cap, the house man, had to pay back to the men the money that Bolo take away. Cap try to get the police to arrest Bolo, but he could never get anybody to go to the court to witness against Bolo. Everybody was afraid.

'I have to do it myself,' Cap tell Sister Elaine, who he buy from in the market. 'I have to damage Bolo, I have to stop him.'

As he tell Sister Elaine, he really didn't want to get himself in trouble at his age, not after he go through all kinda battle days when gangs of men use to be running around with cutlass and iron bolts. But he couldn't let this thing go on. Old as he was, he was still a man, and anyway if Bolo keep on getting away with what he doing, then every little force-ripe badjohn with two drinks in his head would want to come in with his face screw up in devil and take up the money off the gambling table and walk away.

'Well, you don't have no problem,' Elaine tell him, 'just stop him from coming in your club.' So Cap put a ban on Bolo. He ban Bolo from the club for ten years. So when Bolo enter the club what greet him on the blackboard is:

BOLO BAN TEN YEARS

'Who ban me?' Bolo ask. 'You ban me, Cap?' (And I telling the story just as Cap tell Sister Elaine and Sister Elaine tell me – I ain't making one cent profit.)

'The Committee,' Cap say. 'The Committee ban you. You can't be coming in here and taking up people money like a joke, so we ban you. That is the rules.'

'Who ban me? Who is the Committee?' Bolo ask the men sitting down gambling at the table. 'Who say I can't play card here?'

Nobody answer.

'Cap, how you could say the Committee ban me when you ain't have no Committee here?'

Cap didn't say nothing. Bolo stand around and then he put money on the table to make a bet. The men hesitate a little, but afterwards they begin to bet him. When he lose, he take up the money they had on the table and went.

'Who will go witness for me?' Cap ask, but by that time Cap know what he was doing. For Cap had a plan.

Nobody want to go.

'Good,' Cap say. 'Good.'

'I not calling the police,' Cap say. 'And I not paying back the money Bolo take away.' And Cap take out his cutlass from below the table and, he tell Elaine, he was ready for anybody.

'You can't do that, Cap,' they say. 'This is a licence club, and if a man put down money on the table and somebody come and take it, the house must pay. The house is responsible.'

'And you not responsible?' Cap ask. 'You all not responsible?'

And men cuss and grumble whole night, but Cap didn't budge and eventually the men settle down. After that whenever Bolo come into the club, the men take up their money and walk away. When he leave they begin to play. When Bolo see that he laugh.

Just as he terrorise the men, Bolo terrorise women. He didn't have to force them, he just call to them and they go with him. Everybody 'fraid Bolo. No, not everybody. But then people say that Charleau crazy.

It will take three Charleaus to make one Bolo. Charleau use to be a mason with the County Council until they fire him because, they say, he was drunk on the job too often, though what people say is that the real reason for losing his job is that he had start to talk out against Ivan Morton. That was Charleau. He had to give him opinion if it kill him and he had suffer for that so often that he reach the stage where he couldn't help himself from saying what he have to say. One night in Mitchell snackette Bolo start a argument with Barber Sonny and cuff him down when Sonny answer him. Charleau was there.

'You wrong,' Charleau tell Bolo straight to his face. 'Barber Sonny ain't do nothing for you to hit him.'

Bolo turn on Charleau and box him in the face.

'You wrong, Bolo,' Charleau say again and again Bolo box Charleau. This time he knock him to the ground.

Charleau get off the floor, spit out blood and stand up in front of Bolo and say it again, 'Bolo you wrong! You wrong! You wrong!' And when Bolo hit him, he remain right on the floor and with blood in his mouth, he scream over and over again, 'You wrong! You wrong! You wrong!' And he cuss Bolo with every bad word he could remember.

'You wrong!' he shout in Bolo face when he was on his feet again.

'Come and take a drink with me,' Bolo say.

'I don't want your drink,' Charleau tell him. 'I ain't no friend of yours,' Charleau say.

People in the snackette was expecting Bolo to really beat up Charleau but Bolo didn't touch him again. In fact, after a time the two of them get to be friends and Charleau was one man who could tell Bolo what he think to his face.

But in Bonasse we didn't have many like Charleau; so Bolo go on doing, doing, building up his fame until Bonasse – not Bonasse alone, the whole island get to know his name. Even the police had a respect for him, and it would be like they was apologizing when they had to go and tell him that they had a warrant to arrest him. If Bolo feel like going with them, he go; if not, he tell them straight he ain't coming, and the police turn around and pretend that they didn't see him.

After a time we begin to treat the whole thing as a kinda joke, and wherever you go you could hear somebody telling about Bolo adventures like it was something from the movie screen. I hear the story about the time Soogrim, a young police constable just out of training and hot for his first arrest, find himself with a warrant to arrest Bolo. And Soogrim, poor boy, strange to the district, don't know the man he going to arrest, jump on his bike, and ride up to where Bolo living and stand up in the road and call out Bolo name. Bolo was inside cooking. He look through his window and see this little police fellar alone with his bicycle, and his broomstick legs and knobbly knees in his short pants. Bolo shout at him, 'Who is you who calling my name?'

'I have a warrant to arrest you,' Soogrim tell him.

'Arrest me? You know who I is, boy? Arrest me? They send you for me?'

Bolo get in a rage that they should send this little raw police for him. He want to know if the police in Bonasse lose respect for him.

'Look,' he tell the boy, 'go back to the station and tell the sergeant to send some real police for me. Tell him to come with guns and a jeep and don't ever send a little police like you here again.'

Soogrim reach the police station trembling, give the sergeant the message and the sergeant order out the jeep and he and four police gone to Bolo house. By the time the jeep reach Bolo, he was eating.

'I am eating,' he tell them. 'Wait.'

And the sergeant and his men with their rifles wait on him.

'Good,' Bolo say, when he look outside and see them. That time he was finish eating. 'Good! I thought you lose respect for me.' He lock his door and go down the steps and into the van waiting for him.

There was all kinda stories about Bolo. They say he sell his soul to the devil so that nobody could beat him in a battle. They say it didn't make sense shooting him because no ordinary bullet could kill him. And, believe me, it look as if all the stories was true because is not one time only that people try to kill Bolo and he get away free.

Bascombe, the forest guard, catch him in his house with his wife, shoot point black at him, miss, the shot graze him, take away a piece of his right ear. Yet it was Bascombe who spend three weeks in the hospital after Bolo grab him. Sam Roberts son, the one who afterwards stowaway to Venezuela, had a knife to Bolo throat one night in a dance in the school. Bolo snatch the knife, break it – break the knife with his two hands – and had young Sam Roberts jumping through the upstairs window to save his life.

And so he was going, going with this recklessness and vexation and wickedness boiling up in him, as if they put him so, as if he had to go, go, go until some great calamity stop him, until he kill somebody and the hangman take him, because it didn't look as if anybody natural could kill him.

As I say, everybody know that a calamity had to fall down on Bolo one day, but when it happen, wasn't he alone suffer; and if we learn anything from all of it, is to see ourself better who we is and what we do to make a man like Bolo what he turn out to be.

9 The Calamity

It was the week after Joyce wedding; she and Clyde decide they can't live without one another, so Clyde write a letter and Bee answer and they married.

The ceremony was in the Anglican church because Clyde is Anglican and the two children want a church wedding. They want their marriage to receive a blessing and we couldn't do it in the Baptist church where Bee himself coulda say the words, because we is still illegal and illegitimate and our ministers don't have the authority to marry anybody – these is the things we still have to bear in this country in that year – but we bear it; and Bee walk down the aisle of the Anglican church tall, a man, with his tie and suit and his daughter on his arm like a princess, in her veil and crown and gloves and high heel shoes. Winston was there from Point Fortin with some friends from the place where he was working, and Bee sister Philomen, and my brother from Arima, and my cousin Shirley from San Fernando. But Taffy ... we didn't hear a word from Taffy. I write him a letter through his uncle but not a word, though John Jeffry, a loader working on Mr Palmer truck that carry goods down to Port of Spain market every Thursday, say he see Taffy by the corner of Prince and George Street one day and went over the talk to him, so I know that at least he alive, but he miss a good fête. We had Hillman band playing and the people from the village full up the house and overflow to the tent in the yard, and thank God rain didn't fall because a lot of people was out in the yard, and Mr Ambrose take the wedding picture, and with drinks and the cake that Clyde mother bake and I bake and the presents that people bring, not big presents, just nice little things, and everybody kissing Joyce and shaking Clyde hand and Bee giving a speech and cousin Shirley, who come from San Fernando all dress up in her fine clothes and her bangles and gold chain, sing a song and people dance and my brother Randolph get so drunk he lie down in the middle of the floor with a smile on his face and we had to pick him up and put him inside on one of the beds.

Yes, it was the week after all that excitement, and I just finish cleaning up and Shirley gone back and Rudolph and Irene and her children all gone and things fix back how they was and the place quiet now because Joyce ain't home again to keep me company. Three o'clock in the day the other two children still in school, so I there alone in the kitchen this big bright day, resting myself on the bench a little, thinking about Joyce, a woman now with home of her own and a man to cook for and keep clean and hold and console when things get stiff and is nothing in the world but a woman softness to ease his pain, and about Taffy who I can't see for money or love, and about how sweet it is to get together with friend and family and have a time with drinking and dancing and everything and I dance too at the wedding – oh, is to see me reeling and spinning. So now I back to face the times with jobs hard for people and the price of everything in the shop and the market going up, up, up like one of those American balloons in the sky, and I don't know what we would do if we didn't have the garden to give us some plantains and yams. All about people bawling but only a few talking out, saying that black or no black Ivan Morton ain't doing what he suppose to do to ease the sufferation of people, but most can't say it though they feeling the pinch cause they have a son in a little job, they have a daughter who want to get a passport to go away, they don't want to lose favour with Ivan Morton and his people.

So I alone home this day and the green sun coming through the window and the crazy breeze making the coconut trees sway and dancing the mango leaves and I, resting there on the bench, feeling the drowsy afternoon rocking me to sleep, hear this voice calling in the yard, calling in the yard, and when I get up and look out I see leaning on the mango tree, like a dog that get run over by a car and manage to limp home, Brother Primus looking small and weary and frighten.

'Brother Primus,' I say, for though he ain't a member of the church again – he leave us that year when the authorities turn on the pressure strong and the police was really hounding us down and he join the Anglican church where it safe to bring up his two girl children proper without having to worry that the police going to bust their heads for praising God – he is still one of us.

'. . . Brother Primus,' I say, for in any case when trouble take somebody you don't stop to ask them what is their religion. 'Brother Primus, what happen?'

'Sister Eva,' he say, and his voice coming from far down in his belly, 'Sister Eva . . .' And he stand up there, a small thin man with his head lean to one side and his mouth half-open and his eyes looking at me as if he forget where he is and what he here for. I stand up there in front him and the mango tree wondering that could weigh down and confuse Primus so, for I know Primus. Primus is the last man in the world you would expect to see in any trouble. Primus don't argue with nobody, he will never say to your face he disagree, and I can't think of one person in Bonasse who was ever his enemy. For years he work in the Public Works Department on the road gang and the only time he fall out with anybody was when the Public Works wanted to give him a promotion. That time the old foreman, Johnny Carterman, had the stroke and die, and because Primus had more service than anybody else they decide to give him the foreman job. Primus turn it down because a foreman had to be a foreman, had to see that a man work and if a man didn't work he had to make the man work or fire him or do something; but Primus didn't want to be on bad terms with nobody, so he give up the promotion.

He was a hard-working man though, and save his money and when his wife die of blood pressure he alone bring up the two girl children. He never look for another wife and though he use to go often and spend a night or two by Mattie Simpson, he just didn't want to have problems between she and his two girl children, so he live with them alone in the house he build near Richardson junction. A ordinary man with no special name except that he was on good terms with everybody. On Friday he would go in the shop and take a drink, one, just so nobody could say that he was stingy, and he would buy a drink for his friends and take one himself but he didn't stay around long to get into any argument, and if argument come up while he was drinking, he would agree with both sides and next thing you know, Primus gone home. Sunday evenings he go to see cricket in the savannah; any side the crowd like – that was his side. He had nothing to do with politics, was never sick or drunk or in debt, so you could understand my surprise when I see Primus in my yard three o'clock in the day with tears on his face like he gone stupid and forget what he come here to say.

'Brother Primus!' And I raise my voice at him so he will know where he is and come back to himself.

'I want to see Brother Bee,' he say, his weak voice sticking in his throat.

'Bee not here, Brother, but you could come and sit down and wait on him if you care to.'

He nod his head and walk and sit down on the front steps near the mango tree. He sit down there with his head bend down, the flesh on his face trembling and his eyes watching across the land of coconut trees. He's a old man. And Primus younger than Bee.

'You will take some coffee?'

And I didn't know if he say yes or if is no he say when he answer me, but I bring the coffee for him anyhow. He sit down there holding the hot cup in his two hands as if he don't know is something to drink.

'Sister Eva, why? What . . .?' And he struggling to talk. 'Sister Eva . . . why? What I do that this trouble should come and fall on me? I don't drink, I don't gamble, I don't do no harm to nobody. Why this thing should come and happen to me?'

And I quiet, listening now, wondering if he not feeling the hotness of the cup in his hands and why he wouldn't drink the coffee.

And he talking: '. . . I can't fight. I not a badjohn. Last month I was fifty-two and in my days not a man could say Primus hurt one grain of hair on his head . . . and this trouble come to me.'

'Brother,' I say, 'trouble miss people but trouble don't pass nobody.'

'. . . And my daughters . . . my daughters, they don't do nobody nutten.'

'Your daughters?' Because last week the girls was at the wedding dancing and looking pretty. 'What happen?'

'Bolo,' he said. 'Bolo gone with my two daughters.'

I sit down. I bend down my head for, yes, this is trouble.

There on the steps he tell me the story: how midday Monday he going home for lunch in the hot sun and see Bolo coming up the road with his head tall and his face serious and his hands swinging, walking in the middle of the road like if the whole village is his own and if another man want to pass he would have to ask his permission. And that same time his daughter, Muriel, the smaller one, seventeen years old, not a child again but a young woman with breasts and flesh on her bones, come from the standpipe by the side of the road carrying a bucket of

116

water on her head and her body swinging free and Bolo coming up the road rest his eyes on the girl, watch her, and turn and look at Primus.

'Primus, I want that girl,' he tell Primus.

'You want that girl?' And Primus think Bolo making a joke.

'I want that girl,' he say.

'Well, what I could tell you,' Primus say, still thinking is a joke, 'Well, you name Bolo and, yes, if the girl want you ... if ...'

'I want the girl, Primus,' he say, and he serious now, like ... like is not a joke.

'Bolo, you know I will give you anything,' Primus tell him. 'But this is my daughter, man. I can't give her away like a cow or a goat.'

'I not good enough for your daughter? That is what you saying?' Bolo ask him.

'How I could say such a thing, Bolo,' Primus say. 'But this girl, she's a young girl, she ain't reach to age yet, ain't ready yet for a husband. I can't let her go so.'

And Bolo stand up there, Primus say, like a lord in front of him, his face serious and his eyes looking down from his height, and no softness in his face. So when Primus see that he waiting, and not to vex him, Primus say, 'But I have another daughter. She's to age. I have another one, you could go and talk to her and if she consent to go with you, okay.'

'The other one is big,' Primus tell him. 'You could come inside the house and see her.'

So Bolo go inside with Primus and Primus call Celestine, his other daughter. She don't like it, but Primus talk to her – after all, she have twenty-three years already and, well, she is a good solid girl. She's a woman and he's a man, so he let Bolo take her. 'I let Celestine go with him, Sister Eva. She take her things and that same evening he take her and go. Okay, I say. She's a woman and he's a man. Okay. If is so it is to be, let it be so.'

'But how you could do that to the girl?' I ask Primus. 'How?' He bend down his head.

'So now you want her back again?' I say.

'Sister Eva, today the smaller girl, Muriel, go to see her sister, Celestine, and . . . and Bolo keep her too . . . I say okay, take Celestine. Take her. She's my own flesh and blood, but she's a woman, take her. Now he take Muriel and lock her up in the house too.'

'Bee coming in a while, Brother Primus.'

So Bee come home and find Primus on the front steps with his shoulders dropping like a fowl that get it wings beat down in a heavy rain, and his face ugly with his pain. And Bee, with his head bend down and his foot shaking as if he working a sewing machine, sit down and listen to Primus story, and even after Primus finish telling it Bee still sit down there as if a burden fall on his shoulders that he must gather up his strength to lift. I offer Bee some coffee. 'No,' he say, then he get up with this world of heaviness on him and a anger too. 'You and Bolo, both of you crazy,' he say. 'Stop your crying and let's go and see if we find Bolo.'

Bee meet Bolo sitting down on the top step in front his little wooden house where he live alone now that his mother dead, with a gun across his knees and his back bend forward a little and one hand propping up his chin, as if was ages he there waiting for them to come to him. And Bee know that time that this thing between them wasn't just Primus daughters and Primus trouble: Bee know that this is the battlefield that Bolo bring the village to.

'Bolo, we come to talk to you,' Bee tell him.

'Talk,' Bolo say, 'I will listen.'

'This thing you do . . . this thing you do is more than over-bearing. This conduct is something we can't accept. You been going on for a long time now, doing what you like, taking what you want, and nobody stop you. I can't believe you think that nobody don't care what happen. I can't believe you think that you will go on go on and nobody will ever tell you nothing. And why you do these things? Because you strong? And you know the jail and people 'fraid you? Because you is big bad Bolo?'

'Yes, because I is Bolo,' Bolo say.

'And because you is Bolo you don't care about people? You don't care about nobody? You forget that you is a human?'

'The Yankees do as they like with your daughters and you thank them, the police hound you down like beast and brutalise you and arrest you for worshipping your God in your religion and you don't lift a hand against them, the big shots in this island have you catching hell to make a living, you don't open your mouth; but me, I, Bolo, I take a girl to live with me and you talking as if I is the devil.'

'Because you is one of us,' Bee tell him.

'I is one of you?'

'Because you is one of the people,' Bee tell him. 'Because you is a warrior we look to to protect us. And what happen? You is the very one that come now to brutalise people. Is the same thing with Ivan Morton. I work to put Ivan Morton in the Council and instead of changing the law to make us free to worship in our religion, he gone up in Richardson mansion to live his own life like a whiteman. And what is his programme? He want us to be civilize . . .'

'You never put me in no Council,' say Bolo. 'You never do nutten for me.'

'You was a born warrior,' Bee tell him. 'You was a king. Nobody didn't have to put you up nowhere, you was there already. Now look what you come to . . .'

'I want to be a man too,' Bolo say. 'I want to be a man.'

'And to be a man is to brutalise your own people? To be a man is to take Primus two daughters to live with you?'

'People? We ain't no people, Bee. A people does know what they doing. A people does know why they getting up in the world on a morning. A people does be going somewhere ... Where you going to that I could, if I want to, go with you? Tell me, Brother Bee.'

'How we could be a people when men like you and Ivan Morton doing the things you do?' Bee tell him.

'No, Brother Bee, no. I don't see anybody doing any different. Everybody living for theyself. They hustling and killing one another to get a job, kissing the big shot backside to survive. That is the people? The only difference is that some have more strength and some have more power. A people does fight for something. What we fight for? Kill Prince, I tell you when he come to attack the church, and what you do? Now it sick my stomach to see what the church come to; so don't come here and tell me 'bout people. What people, Brother Bee? But you come against Bolo. You come against me.'

'We come to talk to you,' Bee tell him. 'We come to ask you to let the girls go.'

'I ain't letting go nobody. You want the girls?'

'Yes,' Bee tell him.

'Then, you have to take the girls from me.'

'But nobody don't want to fight you,' Bee tell him. 'Nobody don't want to be your enemy. We is all one people and we go through the same troubles, and if we have a little understanding, we have to reason. We have to talk so we understand one another.'

'I want you people to be against me,' Bolo say, and his voice. Bee tell me, was a terrible cry. 'I want you to be my enemy. I want you to come and take these girls from me.'

'We make mistakes, all of us,' Bee tell him. 'We have weak moments, all of us. But who is to make up a people if those who have the strength, those who have the knowledge, if they don't show the way by what they do? Eh, Bolo? You can't expect us to leave these girls with you and go on as if nothing happen,' Bee tell him. 'You can't expect me to close my eyes to this thing that you do, as if we ain't have no shame, as if we not men again.'

'You will have to take these girls from me,' Bolo say.

'You know we could bring the police for you,' Bee tell him.

'Police!' And he was on his feet that time and his eyes was two red coals. 'Bring police here and I will kill everybody, myself too.'

'Bolo, you have to be reasonable,' Bee tell him.

'If you want, keep the big one, but give back Muriel,' Primus say.

'You better go, both of you. When you ready to take the girls come and meet me. I will be here waiting for you.'

'We have to kill him,' Bee say, home now, the two of us on our own steps, after Bee finish tell me what happen. 'We can't put the police on him, and talking wouldn't do.'

'Killing, Bee? Why you don't just call the police for him? They know how to deal with these things. Is their job,' I tell Bee.

'No. This is something weself have to do. We have to show him we is a people.'

And Bee wasn't vex. He was just saying the words with a calm sad gentleness, not sudden, but as if he had turn them and twist them in his mind. '*We* have to kill him.'

'Kill?' I ask Bee. 'You know what you saying? Kill? Killing will show him that we is a people?' And God knows, I frighten, 'cause in all my years with Bee I never hear him talk 'bout killing. And I know his voice. I know he mean what he telling me.

'You can't get the men together, if that is what you want, and go and sit down and talk to him and let him see reason?'

'That will depend on what he do. We have to chastise him. We have to go against him with strength and anger. We have to

121

show him that one man can't stand up against a people.'

'And out of everybody, you choose Bolo out to do this to?' I ask Bee.

'He choose out himself,' Bee tell me. 'He choose out himself for this.'

And I didn't say nothing. I wasn't sure I understand: 'He choose out himself, you say?'

'Yes. To be the sacrifice. To be the one terrible enough and strong enough and close enough to our heart to drive us to take up our manhood challenge that we turn away from for too long. He push us and push us until we have to stand up against him.'

'So,' and I was amazed, 'so, he doing this for us?'

'You could say so, yes.'

I get silent.

'So you see why we can't bring the police in? This is something between the village and Bolo,' Bee say.

I nod my head.

'So you know what I have to do now?' Bee ask.

'You have to go in the village and get the men to go against him,' I say. And rightaway a fear strike me: the men? Who he will get to go with him?

'Who you will get?' And I talk slow and my voice careful to keep it from trembling.

'We will get the men,' Bee say, and as he say it, his eyes see mine and the fear in it. 'We will get people,' he say, firm, his voice, but in his eyes, he wondering.

That same night Bee leave home, without eating, to go for these men. I try to wait up for him. I sit down in the rocking chair thinking, hoping, and I drop off to sleep and in my dream I was in a strange place where there was a mountain and Christ was on the cross and I was there with a stone in my hand and he was bleeding and I was alone and I ask him what to do and he say, 'Take these girls from me.' And I hear footsteps inside the house and it was Bee. And I frighten to ask him anything. That night I didn't sleep.

The morning come and we get up early and Bee put on his clothes and I go in the kitchen to make some coffee, and while I there I hear the dogs barking and then I hear somebody calling. It was Charleau and Mr Buntin, and I invite them in the kitchen and I give them some coffee, and they all drink coffee and nobody saying nothing. Then, Beep! Beep! Beep! I look through the kitchen window and see in the trace in front the yard, the sergeant of police coming out of the police jeep.

'Bee!' I say.

'I see,' Bee say. 'Primus with them too.'

The sergeant call out to Bee and Bee go out to talk to him. The policemen come out the van, six of them, and Primus is there with them. The sergeant talk to Bee. The sergeant is a tall bony red-skin man with long long hands and knotty knees above his putties, and his head shape like a mango vert seed. He stand up with his weight on one foot, easy, loose, lazy almost, with a look on his face that you could take for a smile; and he talking to Bee, moving his hands in that sure lazy way, like he know already just what he going to do no matter what Bee say. And Bee, short in front of him, stand up with his back straight, his face turn up, listening, shaking his head slow, not lazy, but with patience as if he know what he know too. But the sergeant is the one with authority and he keep on talking, his hands waving in long lazy moves as if Bee disagreeing don't mean too much to him. Then he stop talking, and now, by the way he holding his head, I guess Bee telling him something; still, on the sergeant face is this smile that mean 'okay, you talk, I only listening.' And Primus is there between the two of them, looking from one face to the other. Now he start talking, and when he finish talk, he bow his head and Bee was standing up straight and still. Then the sergeant lift up his two hands with the fingers spread open and hold them up in front of Bee.

Then they stop talking, and I see Bee coming.

'What happen?' I ask Bee. 'I thought you say you didn't want the police to interfere.'

'Primus. Primus call them.'

'Primus?'

'We can't worry with that now. We waiting on the rest of the men. The sergeant give me ten minutes for the men to come. If they don't come he will go and arrest Bolo.'

'Maybe I could go to the village and see if I get the men,' Mr Buntin say.

'They know we have to meet here,' Charleau tell him.

'We will wait the ten minutes then,' Bee say.

'Well, invite the police for a cup of coffee. We have plenty.'

The police come and they drink the coffee, and then it was time. Bee get up. The sergeant get up.

'Mr Dorcas, you all could ride with us,' the sergeant say.

Bee look at Buntin and Charleau, 'Okay,' he say.

It was a cool morning and quiet with a light drizzle coming down and the sunshine dazzling through the falling rain bringing all its colours into the day this early morning. I stand up at the kitchen window and watch Bee go in the blue police jeep, and I remain there at the window long after he gone, watching outside, watching the marigolds in a corner of the yard with their yellow flowers like turn up parasols catching the white rain and above them the coconut tree with its trunk straight and its head leaning to one side in the slow wind and its branches stretch out like two arms making a cross under the sky, and coming down the road is Brother Christopher and his son in their donkey cart rolling along on their way to the piece of land Brother Christopher have in the trace behind the Estate, and Brother Christopher wave good morning and I say good morning and he pass on holding the reins of the slow donkey cart with the little boy at the back of the cart with his feet hanging over the side and his hands holding two banana leaves over his head to shelter the rain. I stay there by the window forgetting time, forgetting everything and a ripe mango fall from the tree and the blackbirds hop on the fence and start pecking its flesh and the chickens come out in the yard and chase the blackbirds away and they hop back on the fence making their squawking cry and putting up their wings like they going to fly but not flying. Then Christopher donkey bray and I go inside and kneel down and pray. And even while I was praying the police jeep would already be in front Bolo house.

They park the jeep. They walk up the hill into the yard, with the sergeant in front walking careful on the slippery grass with his long arms stretch out to balance him, to keep him from sliding down the hill, going his easy jovial way so that if you don't know him you would think he's a clown, saying to Bee and Primus and Mr Buntin walking by him, 'Bolo need steps in this place,' and in the same casual way calling, 'Bolo! Bolo!' And Bolo would come to the window and when he see them – the sergeant and the six policemen and Bee and Primus and Charleau and Mr Buntin – he would shut the window and the front door would open and he would be standing there, as Bee would say, stiff, straight, his legs spread apart and his chest up and mouth gruff, his gun in his hands, not saying nothing, just watching with his eyes, Bee say, and the sergeant stand up below the steps in front the door looking at him, 'Bolo, I want to have a few words with you.'

But Bolo is not looking at the sergeant, he looking at Bee, Bee say, not even with vexation but with scorn.

'So you bring police for me, eh, Brother Bee. You bring police for me,' he say, not questioning it but fixing it as a fact in his brain. And he spit on the ground.

'I have a complaint,' the sergeant say, in his slow, lazy way. 'This man daughters . . .' and he point a finger at Primus.

And Bolo face was the saddest face you ever see, Bee tell me.

'They bring *police* for me,' he say over and over again in that soft voice full of astonishment, looking around him as if suddenly he want to sit down and cry.

'I come for the girls,' the sergeant say, very soft, very soft with his kinda smile on his face and moving his hands in this slow lazy casual way.

'These is the people you bring to face me? These is the men of the village? This is the people?' Bolo ask Bee. And Bee looking at him not saying nothing, glancing at Primus for Primus who know the truth to say something, but Primus stand up there trembling ain't saying nothing.

'You come for the girls?' Bolo turn now to the sergeant. 'Then you come to kill me,' he say in a matter-of-fact way.

'I come for the girls,' the sergeant say, moving to his side a little so Bolo would be standing a good target for the two police behind him with rifles.

'You come for the girls,' Bolo say in another voice, a new voice full with a calm vexation and a promise of battle.

And Bolo back through the door into the house and when he come out again he stand up on the top steps with the two girls in front him.

'Come and take them,' he say, and his voice and person is a challenge to the police now, to the law and the governor and the queen, as if his mind make up and his accounts settle and he ready, 'Come and take them.'

And the girls stand up there stiff frighten like two dolls that can't talk, the big one with her breasts outline under her dress that the rain was wetting and her eyes looking straight out in front her at nothing and the small one with her head bend down and her hands fold in front her. And Primus crying now so you could hear him, like he strangling, and his face ugly and the rain on his face. And the sergeant stand up loose, lazy with that half smile on his face, but his eyes alive, watching everything.

'Bolo,' Bee say.

'I don't want to hear you, Bee. Not you.'

'Bolo, I didn't bring police for you,' Bee say.

And Primus watching the girls and wiping his eyes with the back of his hands, and the six policemen spread out in a circle with their guns on Bolo who stand up on the steps with the girls in front him.

'Bolo, I am coming for the girls,' the sergeant say, cool, easy, casual, as if he was asking for a drink of water.

'No,' Bee say. 'No. I will go. Let me go for them. Let me go.'

'Don't come up here, Brother Bee,' Bolo say, as Bee make a move to the steps. 'Don't come up here, none of you.' And Bolo is holding his shotgun against the back of the smaller girl, the one with her head down, and on his face is this terrible sadness and rage and water is in his eyes that wasn't from the rain.

'Bolo, you ain't crazy,' the sergeant say, not moving, just shifting his weight on his loose lanky body like a stickfighter who next move you can't guess.

And Bolo stand up there.

Then Bolo, as if he find that he is too much a man to hide behind the girls, even now there with the police and their guns, move out from behind the sisters, his gun in his hands, and his face holding that calm weariness, and he tall there on the steps with the gun in his hands as if he don't know who to point it at, for he don't want to shoot the girls, Bee think, although, Bee say, you can't be sure because when a man reach a certain state you can't tell what he will do. So I guess the police had the same thought too, and as he move and stand up there in the open – and Bee say he don't really know how it happen, he don't know if is Primus who move or the daughter, or, if the police, seeing Bolo stand up there with the gun in his hand, get frighten and decide that is better they shoot first and find out

127

later – what exactly happen nobody could tell even after. A shot fire off and another shot and, Bee say, Bolo pitch forward tumble down the steps and when he come to rest his head was lying at the foot of the steps and his body was sprawl over the ground, with his two feet close together and his arms stretch out as if the shot sting him and fling out his hands so he would come to lie down with his arms stretch out.

And in that same second with the other shot still echoing, the girl, the small one, Muriel, fall down on the steps and roll and come to rest with her face down near by Bolo right hand, and she didn't move, and Bolo didn't move either, and the two of them was dead.

Then the rain really fall. I mean, it had rain. Rain, rain, rain with thunder and big lightning flashing.

I, home, hear the news from Trotman who come running up the road bawling above the rain; and people was leaving their house and running down the street to go and see what happen, and I take my pot off the fire and tie my head and put on Bee old jacket and pelt out in this big rain and lightning to go down the road to where Bolo living to see for myself what happen and if anything happen to Bee.

By the time I reach there the place would be jampack with people and the police did already block off the street so nobody could go up in Bolo yard to see what happen. We stand up there in the rain, looking up at the house as if we can't believe, as if it ain't true, as if a gunshot can't kill Bolo. We stand up there with the thunder rolling and the lightning flashing, talking in hush hush voices, looking up the hill as if we expect to see him come striding down the hill from his house with his tall terrible walk and his eyes and the rain falling on his face, and we would stand up there watching the police busying themselves in the rain, and bit by bit our faith would give away and among us people was beginning to say, he really dead. And one man, Innocent, the stickfighter, say with a kinda sigh, 'He wouldn't rest until he kill somebody, he will rest now. He dead.'

And Mitchell was there looking like he waiting for somebody to congratulate him.

I see Bee coming through the crowd, tired, groggy, his face ashes, his eyes wandering, looking from face to face as if in some face there is something that he want to see.

'Bee,' I say, 'what happen?'

'We didn't kill him,' he say.

'What happen?'

Later he would tell me.

It was time to go home and we went home and all the way Bee mumbling, 'We didn't kill him.'

And, yes, we didn't kill Bolo. His death didn't take away from us the burden that was ours and that is ours even today. His dying ain't solve no problem for us. It just give us the chance, if we so weak to take it, if we so dead to hold on to it, to put aside our human challenge and blame it all on Bolo, make him the victim and the sacrifice, make him Christ who they let the soldiers crucify on the cross because they didn't care enough, because it was easier for Christ to bear the sins of the world than for people to take upon their own self in their own life the burden that is theirs from being human in the world and come against wickedness and come against the Roman soldiers and come against the shame that people living in and come against the principalities and powers who shower down rocks for bread and who brutalise us every day. It just give us the chance to pretend that his death solve the problem. As if when Christ die on the cross every one of us don't have to come and in our own living bear our own cross and die on it again.

'They don't care,' Bee say, his grief stifling him. 'People don't care. Bolo was bigger. He care.'

We was there at Bolo wake next night with Mr Buntin and

129

Charleau and Marshall, and out in the road the men was dancing the bongo and we could hear the songs ringing clear across Bonasse, and in the house people was singing hymns. We was on a bench outside near where some fellars was gambling. And Mr Buntin was remembering with many sighs and a kinda pride in his voice, a kinda sadness and a choking: he was remembering Bolo when he come out of jail and the things he wanted to do and how he wanted a girl to married and some land to build a house on and to be a man. 'He was looking for his life,' Mr Buntin say.

'People don't care for their own self,' Bee say.

'And who is Bolo?' Mr Buntin say. 'Who is Bolo, Bee?'

'But we didn't even go against him,' Bee say.

Mr Buntin sigh, Mr Buntin shake his head and reach out his hand and touch Bee and hold Bee hand. 'We is like a people after a shipwreck, Bee. You know, the ship sink and everybody jump in the water and we ain't have no boats and each man have to struggle to save himself; that is we, Bee,' Mr Buntin say. 'We not wicked, is just people trying each man to save himself from drowning.'

'Save? But how we could save ourselves alone, Buntin? How we could save ourselves scatter like leaves without a tree to hold on to?'

'But what we have to hold on to, Bee? Ain't they destroy the church? Ain't they make it a crime to worship as Baptist? Ain't they mash up the boats to take us across the sea?'

'And they make it a crime for us to go against Bolo too, eh, Buntin? We don't care, man. We don't care.'

'I tired, Eva. Tired,' Bee say when we was going home from the wake that same night and reach the end of the trace and see across the stretch of darkness that can't hide the shapes of coconut trees the lamp lighting in our house. And I wish I was young again. I wish my hands was soft to cool his forehead and my breasts firm to rest him comfortable.

'Maybe people don't know they care, Bee. Or maybe is just the time, just the time ain't come yet for them to show it. Maybe people need to see what they doing. They need a victory sense, Bee, a feeling that when they stand up against principalities and powers they will win and not be dashing their head against another wall again. People want to live. People care about their living.'

For a while it look like he going to explain something, but he just shake his head, shake his head, 'I tired,' he say.

We walk home, putting our foot down careful, and in the dark raindrops was slipping off leaves and from their little damp places in the bushes frogs was singing their songs, and by my side Bee is a old man walking slow, walking slow.

'I really tired, you know,' he tell me. And I could hear in his voice the breaking, the cracking, the oldness of his age.

'Tired? You just want a little rest then you back again. People like you don't get tired, Bee. People like you is the pillars holding up the earth. If you get tired the whole world fall down.'

And true to my word, Bee was back again at Bolo funeral next day to preach the sermon in our little church, with the people pack in from the rain. Bee was there in his black gown and his face full of that deep sad knowing, with strength still to preach out of himself, with his tiredness, 'Love ye one another,' with a fierce tenderness and pleading. And I know he was talking to himself too.

In the rain, we bury Bolo. But in my mind I know that he ain't buried. I hope he not buried.

That Sunday they had the whole thing in the papers, with photographs of Bolo and the two girls and Primus, and they had the sergeant picture too in his cap and uniform and the three silver stripes on his arm. They write about Bolo as if he was a beast loose in the village and the sergeant is the hero who take his life in his hands and go and save the girls from slaughter. 'Enemy of the People' they call Bolo. And I can't blame them for there is their office in Port of Spain they know nothing about us or Bolo. What they know? If it wasn't for that killing they woulda never know there is a place in Trinidad call Bonasse.

As Charleau would say later, talking to the men in front Buntin shop down the bay, 'To them we is just clowns digging the ground to grow food for them to eat, milking the cows to get milk for them to drink, fixing the road for their motor cars to run on. Nothing we is; and the only time we get in fashion is when election time come round and they want a crowd of people to clap hands when they make their speech. They want a crowd of fools to argue and fight one another over which one of them going to rule over us.'

And we really blind not to see that to these people we is just a joke that come in fashion once every five years when they come with pen and paper and take our names, promising to bring down the moon and the stars, fêting us on rum and roti so we could ride their car on election morning and mark a X next to their name.

A few months after we finish bury Bolo we would be back in fashion, for it was five years since we had the last election and now one was coming up again.

10 The Church Comes Back

I don't say that Ivan Morton had to be a magician. I don't say that he coulda solve every problem we face him with, but if he have any responsibility to anybody is to we who choose him out as the one man able enough and strong to stand up for us in the Council of the land. And even without grumbling, year in and year out we watch him and wait for deliverance and we hope and hope until hope get thin like malnutrition children and faith dry up like old men skin, getting hard, making scales, and we realize that it ain't make no sense looking to Ivan Morton again.

I ain't talking just about the church – though Bee say the church is the key to everything, that if Ivan Morton can't understand that to free the church is to free us, if he can't understand that the church is the root for us to grow out from, the church is Africa in us, black in us, if he can't understand that the church is the thing, the instrument to make us legal and legitimate and to free him, Ivan Morton, himself too, if he can't understand that, Bee say, then he don't have any understanding of himself or of black people.

But I ain't talking only about the church, for let us say that for whatever reason Ivan Morton really don't understand why in this country we should first want to see ourselves as black, let us say he don't understand that to say Trinidadian or West Indian don't by itself describe our condition, let us say that he don't understand why we want to be Baptist instead of Catholic or Anglican, I want to know what preventing him from seeing us as people. I mean, I want to know what preventing him from seeing that we is people who need a decent health office to go to and sit down comfortable instead of standing up in a line like criminals in the hot sun road waiting for the doctor who come on Tuesday alone, and when you do get a seat is on a hard wood bench like you in jail, and the nurse so rough, you wish you had the money to go to a private doctor where you could sit down and be somebody. I mean, what preventing him from seeing us as a people who want jobs for our children and to be somebody in the world outside the drawers of water and the hewers of wood; what preventing Ivan Morton from seeing that? What is it? What? No, I ain't vex with him, for I don't believe that Ivan Morton with all he do more wicked than any other body, I trying to understand what make him turn out so, or if is a curse put on black people that the very one we choose as leader should turn his back on us.

'Stupid,' Bee say. 'Foolish.'

But stupid don't explain him, not to me. Ivan Morton is a man with intelligence. He must have human feelings. He must remember where he come from and the hell his mother and father see to raise him in this country. He must remember. Stupid don't explain it to me. Unless ... unless is a kind of stupid where you don't know what you doing, where you doing something not deliberate to be wicked but out of some other wanting.

And what he could want so? What any man could want so? Or maybe is as Bee himself say that a man must be a man for himself first before anything. Maybe it was this: trying to be a man for himself in the world first before anything; for even Christ, when he take up the cross, was out of his own self, for his own living first, and we, if we learn anything from his dying, is that every one of us have to be ready to be crucify for his living. Maybe is because he couldn't be black like one of us ordinary Bonasse people and be a man too, because the world wouldn't let him.

'And a little respect?' Bee say. 'A little respect for people is too much to expect from him? You mean we is such jackasses in his eyes that he will come now, knowing that is election time again, to put on this big show, to busy himself all of a sudden, pretending that he trying to do what for all these years in the Council he make no attempt to do. You mean he can't give us at least the benefit of having a little sense to see that this sudden rush to fix roads, this sudden rush to answer applications for land, this sudden rush to put up crash programmes to give a man a job for a week or two is just a trick for the election? Eh? Not even respect? Shame? You mean he lose all shame for himself too so that he come now with all this tomfoolery to face people as if we is fools, puppets to swing, hands to clap and fingers to write X on a ballot to give a vote to him?'

But maybe is true. Maybe Ivan Morton really don't see us as people. Maybe to him we is really nutten. Oh God! Maybe because his manness was so important to him and because we didn't, don't have no world, no world with power where he could be a man in, where his manness could come out legitimate just from being himself (seeing that the church was illegal and we didn't have no school to educate him in, didn't have no roots for him to grow out of and be a man so that even before he was a man he had to leave the church and go to the Catholic school so he could get a chance to make a place for himself in the world). Oh God! Maybe is our own weakness: that because we don't have the power, the strength of our own to hold up our children, to protect them, and keep alive our church for our people to worship in. Maybe is our weakness and not the wickedness of our children that turn them away from us and from their self to try to be something else where they could feel that they is human beings.

'Bee!'

'We choose him to fight,' Bee say. 'To stand up.'

'To stand up alone, Bee? Alone? For if we didn't have the strength, if we didn't have the power, if we wasn't standing up on our own as a people, what was he there standing up for? We is a lot of people but we ain't a people. I mean, Ivan Morton couldn't be a leader because we wasn't a people. I mean, we wasn't the trunk of a tree that grow out from roots to make him a branch that grow out from our body. I mean, we couldn't give him the nourishment to be himself so he could take in the sunlight as a branch do through leaves so that together with the juices from our roots we could produce fruit. Is not a leader we choose, Bee, but a star, a star to be alone.'

'A star indeed,' Bee say, 'without no responsibility to people and so stupid that he don't even know that unless black people is people he cannot on his own be a man, that all the manness that he create with books and position is just a flimsy thing that could break down and crumble any time. Stupid, I tell you.' But me, I don't know. I don't know. Maybe things happen in season, and there is a time for Ivan Morton to be and a time for him to go.

This year the men on Bonasse coconut Estate decide that they wasn't getting enough pay and go to Mr Lightbrown who was now managing the Estate for the owner who live in America, and Lightbrown like the little fool he is draw up his red-nigger self like a peacock who own the world and the Estate is not his at all – he is just a worker there like anybody – draw up himself and tell the men that he ain't have no more money to give them and if they don't want to work they could go home, so that the men, some who work twenty, thirty years for the next-to-nothing Estate pay from under Mr Richardson, decide that they would go on strike until they get a decent pay. And they strike, too, for two full weeks until Lightbrown claim that they set fire to a building on the Estate and call in the police who come with their batons and their guns and their steel helmets and surround the men and prod them and provoke them until a fight break out and they arrest fifteen or twenty of them. In all that Ivan Morton ain't do nutten, so you must understand that this can't sit down well with Bonasse people. And though the strike eventually fizzle out to nutten, with the men going back to work for a extra penny or two, people begin looking at Ivan Morton very different from the years before. Even Brother Oswald who say we wasn't giving the man a chance to do his job was ready now to give up on him.

This year too a restlessness and vexation was gripping Bonasse people, maybe it was Bolo haunting the men from his grave, making them see that you have to care for your own living no matter what the cost, if you going to remain a human being, or maybe the time was ripe for our vexation, for the children was big from that generation of us who was struggling and could take care of theyself and we was ready now to stand up for ourself, or maybe the wickedness tumbling down on us over the years was just too much and we was tired at last and on edge like a man who you wouldn't let rest, who want to sit down and catch his breath and you there prodding him, harassing him until he get so vex and irritated that he ready to fling the last bit of his strength left in him at you and knock you down so you would leave him in peace.

Down at Buntin shop Charleau and Craig and Marshall from the Estate was talking every day and already they was saying that voting for a man didn't make sense anyway. And when Ivan Morton come in the village with his big smile and belly pushing against his jacket, we didn't make a great big fuss over him and even the children didn't run behind his car again. But he have a chance; for running against him is a light-skin mulatto lawyer name de Gannes, and Ramsumir, a Indian doctor who just come back from England.

'They not any better than him, Bee,' Mitchell say, talking to Bee. Mitchell campaigning for him. Well, who could blame him?

And Bee sit there on the front steps with his arms fold across his chest looking across at Mitchell who sit down, his huge body flowing over off the chair, his neck short and thick like the trunk of a tapana tree and his arms sticking out from his body like a stuff up dummy. And Mitchell looking around, his eyes resting everywhere except on Bee face, and he talking in this hoarse gravelly groaning voice, stopping to catch his breath every few seconds as if what he saying is the last true words and you have to catch them before his voice fade away entirely.

'I ain't saying that he do everything, Bee, but he is still our own and if we don't support him, de Gannes or the Indian will come in. You want the Indian to rule you?'

And Bee sit down on the bench with his folded arms and his head lean to one side a little as if he thinking what is the wisest thing he could say, no vexation was showing on his face, and Mitchell still talking in his slow shaky gravelly voice. And then Mitchell stop talking.

'You finish talk Mitchell?' Bee ask in a very pleasant voice.

'Yes.'

'Good.' And Bee unfold his arms and rise up from the bench. 'I have things to do.'

'But Bee. . . ?' Mitchell say, but Bee just stand up there waiting for Mitchell to get off his chair and leave his place.

After Mitchell gone, Bee walk down by the cowpen and take out this new cow that he have now, walk it to the roadside to graze. Through the kitchen window I watch him squat down near the roadside near the cow cropping the grass and he letting the rope slip from his fingers as the cow move on to the good grass and when it move a distance off he get up and follow so he always near to it. And slow now Bee go, his hair greying and his back bending a little from that stiff straightness, that steel that was in him and his eyes looking at the grass and the cow eating as if there is something, a lesson in the grass the cow cropping, and people passing and Bee raising his head and waving his hand: 'Good evening, Brother Rogers, good evening, Sister Smith,' and then going back to watching the cow crop the grass.

I look at Gem and Reggie, I look at Joyce with her belly getting big with her first baby, and Bee there these days grazing the cow and growing grey and the buzzing going on in the village, the men discussing down at Buntin, and these last children, Gem going to high school and Reggie just beginning to work, and if it come to this, if it come to this where we old now, Bee and me, we had some kinda chance to live and we take it and do the best we could and the battle is the children own, for what we could do if the ones to lead the people find that for their own reason they have to turn against the people, what we could do? And Bee there grazing the cow, watching the grass, and I hope he seeing that the grass that the cow crop one day grow back the next day, I hope he seeing this. And I hope the children watching us, watching all that happening, for this is the end of our times, the old times, the hard rock-stone times, and they should look at them well and they should look at their father how he try, how he try through trials and tribulations to be man not for himself alone but how he take up his burden for the people and do what he had to do.

These days my mind jumping all over the place, I thinking things that never come in my head before and Ivan Morton carrying on his election campaign. Every day he in the papers, he opening a show, he attending a bingo, he giving a talk in the library in San Fernando. And now he trying to win us over again, coming through the village saying he giving a scholar-ship to the children, saying he going to raise the pension for the old people; so that is how it come that day that Reggie would put in my hand this newspaper with Ivan Morton picture staring out from the front page.

I look at the picture. I look at the face plump and nice for his age and I go to give it back to Reggie, for I wasn't in a mood to read, it wasn't a nice day for me.

You know when you getting old a day does come in your life when you tired and you feeling a hurting and you don't know which part of your body the pain is in, one of those days when you weary from the years of worrying about the children and your husband and how life going and you looking at things and you can't laugh again for things ain't getting better and you weary and your shoulders drooping and your neck can't bear your own head weight, and sudden you realize that after all these years, after all these years you still here and so much to do and you can't do it, so much to save and if you could save yourself alone in this world that by itself is enough miracle. It was a day like that with me.

I sit down on the front steps in the sunshine catching the little breeze that blowing 'cross the yard and swinging the ripening mangoes on their stems, and I combing my hair, plaiting it in rows – long time ago, so long, I use to take out the grey hairs when they was few – and watching the chickens scratching in the yard and the stripe butterflies zigzagging like kites that can't fly well over the hibiscus hedge where the flowers unfolding like red parasols and the bees rushing from flower to flower and listening to the hens cackle as the cocks strut and the wind blow and thinking that maybe is a good thing that Taffy gone and Winston gone and thinking that even if we bear what He send like the earth bear the rain and hot sun and the digging and the tramping, even if we bear all the tribulation that rain down on us for generations, is still not enough just to be here to bear and, yes, we bear like the earth we send up things too, we send up flowers, but we have to rise too, we have to rise like the sun rise, we have to shine in a sky, and I don't know why, I feel so good that Taffy with all restlessness in him gone to find things out, secrets, and I would just like to see him, for him to come and sit down by my side and tell me what happening in Port of Spain world, how people going, what they thinking, for old as I is I ain't know nothing. So this is me there on the steps that day when Reggie come home showing me this paper with Ivan Morton picture on the front page.

'Read this, Ma,' he say, pointing to the place below Ivan Morton picture.

'Boy,' I say, 'I feeling tired today. I really ain't have the strength to think about Ivan Morton and his politics. What happen? He going to a conference in England again?'

'Read it, Ma,' he say and he smile, and Reggie have such a smile, and how he will charm those young ladies, how he will charm them.

'You really want me to read it, eh. Okay, go and bring my glasses for me.'

He bring the glasses and I put them on my face and I begin to read the place under the Ivan Morton picture.

'Jeesus! Lord! Boy!' I sit down there with the paper in my hand and my breath gone and I can't breathe and a sorrow and gladness cut through my body like a wind pain. I sit down on the steps with my eyes two rivers at overflow so I can't even see the words on the paper. And so long we wait, so long, so long. 'This . . . this is true, Reggie?'

'Is there in the paper,' he say.

And though I know Ivan Morton will do anything to get us to put him back in the Council, I never believe I woulda live to see the day when the law would pass to make us free to worship God in our way.

'Go. Go and call your father . . . No. Let me go. You might go and shock him like you shock me with this paper.'

Rightaway I forget my weariness and I get all confuse and fussy so I couldn't even find the cloth to tie my head, but I get the cloth and I tie my head, and see me running through the trace to the garden where Bee working that day moulding some tomato trees. I see him there alone in the hot sun, bend over the land with his hoe in hand pulling the earth and piling it up around the young tomato plants with that calm deep patience that make things push up from the darkness of the earth and grow.

'Bee!' And I who talk about exciting him was flying to him with my shoes off and my dress flying and my headtie loose, rushing through the bushes of the trace across the earth to him and he turning, rising from his hoeing and I want to tell him is all right with me and the children, is all right, but my breath gone and I running to him and even when he catch me all I could do is wave the paper and call his name, 'Bee! Bee!'

He look at the paper. He look at me. He look at the paper again.

'Eva,' he say.

'Yes,' I say. 'Yes, Bee. Yes. Yes.'

'Eva,' and he hold me and is I who have to hold him up, and we sit down on the ground together.

'Eva,' he say.

'Yes, Bee. Yes.'

I was happy. And my joy was taller than church bells to see Bee face with the smile bursting out on it like how the sun does come through Bonasse sky in the morning. 'Yes, yes, yes.'

That weekend and for the whole of that next week we publish the news throughout the village so that all those of the congregation who through the years of tribulation had run away would know they could come back to the church to worship as in the old days with hymn singing and bell ringing and hand-clapping and shouting and dancing; and we set aside the following Sunday as the day when we would celebrate our freedom day.

The day come. That morning I get up at five o'clock, with the sun coming up over Bonasse hills, drifting the mist away and sparkling the grass with the dew on it, and with the cocks crowing and the birds singing and Brother Christopher donkey braying, and a nice breeze blowing through the kitchen like Christmas morning. We set the time for the service at ten o'clock so that after we finish with church we would have time to go down to the election meeting that Ivan Morton was holding down in front Mitchell snackette at three o'clock in the day.

And is to see us walking up the street, Bee and me and the children, with Bee in his white gown that he use to say we would have to bury him in because it didn't look like he would get a chance to wear it while he was living, and his head tie with three cloths – white, black and yellow – the yellow signifying the light and the glory of ascension and the white the resurrection and the black the earth that keep us all for all these years, with the shepherd staff in his hand and his sandals on his foot and his head up and his eyes on our little church on the hill between the mango trees that Brother Alfred trim to unhide it from the world, to show it without shame at last to the village.

It was a nice morning for the world and we go through the village, joining our brothers and sisters on their way to the church this happy day.

The church was ready too, with its fresh coat of paint and the flowers around it – the zinnias and marigold and croton and Jacob's coat – showing their colours and smelling nice, and the birds come out on the mango tree and among the flowers to hop and whistle and liven the place with their moving and colour and song.

We go in the church where incense burning and candles lighting in every corner, and at the Centre Post there is the bell and the bowl of flowers with the marigold and roses and croton and fern and the holy water, and on the benches is the sisters and brothers in their colours – the browns and the greens and the whites and the blues – and their faces smiling and their eyes without the strain and fear and waiting for the police to come in.

Then Bee walk and go and stand up on the pulpit and he lift up his voice, and for the lesson he read the psalm that David sing when the Lord deliver him from the hands of his enemies, the psalm that say:

Let us make a joyful noise to the rock of our salvation
Let us come before his presence with thanksgiving
And make a joyful noise unto him with psalms
For the Lord is a great God and a great king above all Gods.

And Bee preach about the tribulation and about the running and dodging and hiding and he preach about the scattering of the people when we scatter like sparks from a fire to die, but we do not die, instead come back again to be here to praise the Lord and to magnify His name. Bee preach and he walk down from the pulpit and kneel down at the Centre Post and take up the bell and ring it to the four corners of the church and he sprinkle water from the bowl of flowers on to the congregation, and nothing . . . nothing happen . . . I mean, the hymn we was singing was coming out our mouth in the Anglican and Catholic way and it wasn't like old times at all.

Sister Ruth get up and she ring the bell and Mother Elaine take up two candles in her hands and they go to the four corners of the church with the candles and the holy water and the ringing bell to unlock the spirits and they went down on their knees and they testify in front the congregation, and we sing hymns and clap our hands but the Spirit wouldn't come. The Spirit wouldn't come, everything we try. It was sorrowful bad. And those of us like Sister Elaine and Mother Ruth and Brother Theophilus who wait all these years was confuse because the Spirit wouldn't come; and Bee was preaching, trying with his voice to call the Spirit, trying with the incense and the lighted candles and the bell and the bowl of flowers and the holy water to bring the Spirit in, but the Spirit wouldn't come that day. It wouldn't come . . . wouldn't come.

And going home from the church now, Bee and me and the children, all of us silent and Bee a little way off in front walking, tramping steady, careful slow, with his silence, with his head up and chest out and hands clasp behind his back as if the hurt and pain was his alone to bear and he could bear it without help if it press him to the ground.

'Your sermon was good, Bee. It wasn't because of your sermon,' I tell him. 'The Spirit just wouldn't come. Maybe we stay too long.'

And Bee walking, one step in front of me, with his calm steady weariness, and above his head the clouds gathering grey and the wind rising in the coconut trees, and as I thinking that he was never going to answer me, he say, 'Too late. It came too late . . . We . . . I shoulda never stop worshipping in the true Baptist way.'

'But is because you care, Bee. Is because you didn't want to take the chance to make them stamp us out altogether. Is because you wanted us to survive, to be here today. Is because you care, man,' I say.

'Care?' Bee say. 'We shoulda fight them, we shoulda kill Prince.'

'Wait, Bee. Wait,' I say. And we stand up, Bee and me and the children. 'Touch me, Bee,' I say.

'Touch you?'

'Yes, touch me. Touch me.'

He look at me like maybe I going crazy but he reach out his hand and hold my own.

'Look, Bee, ain't we here? Look at us, and your son and daughter; ain't we still here? Look at us, Bee, now we could baptise open anywhere in the island and sing and ring the bell and sprinkle water from the bowl of flowers. The Spirit will come back, Bee. We here, we and the children.'